D1553353

Friedrich Hölderlin

Intersections: A SUNY Series in Philosophy
and Critical Theory

Rodolphe Gasché and Mark C. Taylor, Editors

FRIEDRICH HÖLDERLIN

Essays and Letters
on Theory

Translated and Edited by
Thomas Pfau

State University of New York Press

Published by
State University of New York Press, Albany

© 1988   State University of New York

For information, address State University of New York
Press, State University Plaza, Albany, N.Y., 12246

Library of Congress Cataloging in Publication Data

Hölderlin, Friedrich, 1770–1843.
    Friedrich Hölderlin : essays and letters on
theory.

    (Intersections : a SUNY series in philosophy and
critical theory)
    Bibliography: p.184
    1. Hölderlin, Friedrich, 1770–1843—Aesthetics.
2. Hölderlin, Friedrich, 1770–1843—Correspondence.
3. Authors, German—18th century—Correspondence.
I. Pfau, Thomas, 1960–   . II. Title. III. Series:
Intersections (Albany, N.Y.)
PT2359.H2A6   1987   831'.6   87-1882
ISBN 0-88706-558-9
ISBN 0-88706-559-7 (pbk.)

10 9 8 7 6 5 4 3 2 1

Table of Contents

Notes on the Translation

The present translation includes, with the exception of a few minor pieces that do not constitute an attempt at theoretical reflection, all of Hölderlin's essays and fragments on philosophical and poetological matters. With respect to the letters, however, a much greater selectivity proved necessary. Of the 312 letters contained in the Stuttgart edition of Hölderlin's works, only eleven could be included in this translation. Again the central criterion for the selection was their theoretical import. Still, many letters of virtually equal significance remain thus far untranslated, and a more comprehensive translation of Hölderlin's correspondence still remains a challenging and worthwhile task. Although the translation is based on the *Grosse Stuttgarter Ausgabe* of Hölderlin's complete works, the more recent Frankfurter Ausgabe with its contrasting editorial principles has been taken into account whenever philological problems were resolved differently, or where it provides additional information on a given text.

Even for a German reader who may be well accustomed to frequent subordination and long-winded syntax, Hölderlin's prose remains an almost unmatched tour-de-force. With his dithyrambic prose style, reflecting his forever differentiating thinking, Hölderlin obliges his translator to adhere—both at the level of syntax and diction—very closely to his language. Yet those who might take exception with the somewhat ponderous and deliberate subordinations, which will characterize Hölderlin's text in any language, should consider that several of the translated essays were taken down as notes for Hölderlin's own use only. When read as what Hölderlin names "thought experiments," the fragments and essays here translated will certainly afford any reader a unique glimpse into the painstaking task of a theorist's attempt at thinking what Hölderlin never ceased to explore: the category of *difference* in its most primordial senses.

I am indebted to Alexander Gelley (University of California, Irvine), Rainer Nagele (Johns Hopkins University), Timothy Bahti (Northwestern University) and Rodolphe Gasché (SUNY Buffalo) for their encouragement and their helpful criticisms on the manuscript. Thanks are also due to Thomas Reimer (SUNY Albany) for his careful preparation of the manuscript. Most of all, I mean to thank my wife Olga Valbuena, whose loving encouragement, support and advice made the task of translating Hölderlin meaningful even when his text remained obscure.

This book is for our first child, Natalie Juliane.

Buffalo, August 1987

List of Abbreviations

SE = *Stuttgart Edition*, referring to the volumes of the *Grosse Stuttgarter Ausgabe* of Hölderlin's works (cf. Bibliography).

FE = *Frankfurt Edition*, referring to the volumes of the *Frankfurter Ausgabe* of Hölderlin's works (cf. Bibliography).

( ) = parenthetical remarks by Hölderlin.

(*) = Subtext by Hölderlin which is printed in smaller script on the bottom of the page in the SE.

(1, 2, 3 etc.) = Translator's notes.

[ ] = Translator's insertions.

[. . .] = A gap in the text of the manuscript which is observed by the SE.

V, 215 = page break in the SE which is observed in the margins of this translation, and with a vertical bar (|) in the text.

Friedrich Hölderlin: A Chronicle

1770, March 20. Johann Christian Friedrich Hölderlin is born in Lauffen (Swabia).

1772, July. Death of Hölderlin's father and birth of Hölderlin's sister Heinrike (Rike).

1774, October. Second marriage of the mother (Johanna Christiana) to the mayor of Nürtingen.

1776. Hölderlin begins to attend school in Nürtingen, and birth of his step-brother Karl.

1779, March. Hölderlin's step-father dies.

1782. Hölderlin receives private instruction from the vicar of Nürtingen, an uncle of Schelling whom Hölderlin meets in 1783.

1784, October. Hölderlin enters school at the abbey of Denkendorf near Nürtingen.

1786, October. Hölderlin enters the school at the abbey in Maulbronn. Hölderlin falls in love with Louise Nast.

1788, October. Hölderlin enters the protestant seminary at Tübingen. He forms friendship and poetic circle with Ludwig Neuffer and Rudolf Magenau.

1789, April. Hölderlin's engagement to Louise Nast is broken off. He meets the publishers Christian F. D. Schubart and Gotthold F. Stäudlin.

1790, September. Hölderlin passes his *Magister Artium* exam. By October, the young Schelling (1775–1854) enters the seminary, and a close friendship forms between Hölderlin, Hegel (1770–1831) and Schelling.

1791, September. First publication of poetry for Stäudlin's
       Musenalmanach.

1792, May. Hölderlin begins his work on *Hyperion.* He publishes
       more poetry in another almanac of Stäudlin.

1793, September. Hegel leaves the seminary for Bern.
       October. Hölderlin meets Schiller in Ludwigsburg who
       recommends him to Charlotte von Kalb as an instructor
       for her son.

1794, Sustained study of Kant's and Fichte's philosophy, and
       continued work on *Hyperion.* Having travelled with his
       disciple Fritz von Kalb to Jena, Hölderlin is introduced
       to Goethe, Herder, Fichte and Niethammer.

1795, January. After increasing pedagogical problems, Hölderlin
       leaves his position as instructor at the house of von Kalb.
       May. Staying on in Jena, Hölderlin meets Fichte and
       Novalis. Shortly afterwards he departs abruptly and,
       through mediation of his friend Johann Gottfried Ebel,
       obtains a position as an instructor at the house of the
       banker Gontard in Frankfurt.

1796, January. Hölderlin starts his tutoring with the Gontard
       family in Frankfurt.
       April. Meeting between Hölderlin and Schelling, possible
       conception of the "System-Program."
       May. Beginning of the deep attraction between Susette
       Gontard and Hölderlin.
       September. After a long period of unrest due to the war
       between the "Reich" and the revolutionary France, Höld-
       erlin and the Gontard Family return to Frankfurt.

1797, January. Hegel comes to Frankfurt where Hölderlin has
       found a position for him.
       August. While Hölderlin begins his plans for "Empedo-
       cles," the first volume of his *Hyperion* along with several
       poems is published.

1798, Hölderlin is working on the first version of his *Empedocles.*
       September. After a falling-out with the banker, Gontard
       (it is not clear to what extent Hölderlin's relationship

with Susette was known to her husband: cf. *SE*: VI. Letter #165, and VI, 888f.), Hölderlin moves his residence from Frankfurt to the nearby Homburg.

1799, The publication of several Hölderlin poems in Schiller's "Musenalmanach" is reviewed positively by Friedrich Schlegel. Between 1799 and 1800, Hölderlin writes most of his theoretical essays. Hölderlin also completes the second version of his "Empedocles."
October. The second volume of his *Hyperion* appears, and several others of his poems are published in Neuffer's *Taschenbuch*.

1800, June. Hölderlin returns to Nürtingen and subsequently moves to Stuttgart where he lives until December.

1801, January. Hölderlin takes up a position as private tutor in Hauptwil (Switzerland). However, he already returns home by April (poem: "Heimkunft").
December (10th?). Hölderlin travels to Bordeaux, France, in order to take up a tutoring position in the house of Konsul Meyer.

1802, January. Arrival in Bordeaux. However, Hölderlin leaves Bordeaux already by May for reasons unknown. By the time of his return, Hölderlin shows clear symptoms of his mental derangement.
June. Susette Gontard dies after a short illness. With the exception of a travel to Regensburg in September, Hölderlin spends the rest of the year in Nürtingen.

1803, June. Hölderlin meets Schelling once again.

1804, June. Isaac von Sinclair, who has been attending to Hölderlin constantly since his return from France, travels with Hölderlin from Nürtingen to Homburg. A last meeting with Schelling takes place on the way in Würzburg.
Juli. Hölderlin's Sophocles translations are published by Friedrich Wilmans.
August. Hölderlin begins his work as a librarian in Homburg. Following the express wish of Hölderlin, Sinclair assumes responsibility for Hölderlin's wages, etc.

1805, February. Sinclair stands trial for treason against the Kur-
       fürst of Württemberg. Hölderlin is temporarily implicated
       in this plot, but the allegations are not substantiated.
       July. Sinclair is released from prison.

1806, August. Obliged to leave Homburg, Sinclair can no longer
       act as the trustee for Hölderlin.

1807, After a stay of approx. 7 months in the psychiatric ward
       of the Tübingen hospital, Hölderlin is moved to the car-
       penter Zimmer in Tübingen. Hölderlin lives there until
       his death in

1843, on June 7th. Hölderlin dies at the age of 73, having spent
       more than 35 years in his room at the carpenter Zimmer.

Critical Introduction

In sharp contrast to his poetical works, which have been translated several times already, the theoretical writings of Friedrich Hölderlin have received little attention from English and American critics. The English scholarship on his essays is virtually non-existent, and only a few translations of his theoretical writings have been undertaken thus far.[1] While the contemporary debate concerning literary theory in this country has frequently unfolded as a reading of Romantic poetry and poetics and, indeed, has focused on the poet Hölderlin as its most prominent German exponent, Hölderlin's theoretical writings, including some of the most suggestive material for this debate, have rarely been considered as the textual basis for such a discussion.[2]

The omission of this very suggestive material from the discourse of contemporary literary theory may be due to the fact that Hölderlin's essays pose tremendous difficulties to the process of reading as well as translation. Their seemingly cryptic nature, a highly specialized vocabulary, their thematic diversity, and furthermore their long-winded, dithyrambic syntax have in the past provoked critics to discredit them as the products of an "insane mind." However, the assessment of Hölderlin's admittedly difficult writings on the basis of his ill-fated biography cannot but result in the mutual reaffirmation of textual and personal idiosyncrasies, not providing, however, any examination of the essays' proper intellectual thrust. Yet with the majority of these essays having been written between 1794 and 1800, and with the problematic of Hölderlin's "madness" (which, at any rate, did not set in before 1803), still remaining unresolved, an open-minded reading cannot but recognize the essays as theoretical statements of most profound insight. Still, any reading of Hölderlin's theoretical writings will require an extraordinary

1

amount of intellectual patience and persistence; yet, as the following introductory remarks are meant to show, such qualities will certainly be rewarded.

The idiosyncrasies of Hölderlin's prose are both syntactic and semantic, and it is particularly in his so-called "Homburg writings" that Hölderlin makes frequent use of neologisms and develops a single sentence into more than a page. As a result, his writings seem to defy any interpretation that rests on aesthetic or historical contextualization. Yet, as the following introductory remarks are meant to show, it is precisely in response to the specific philosophico-historical debate of his age that what may be called Hölderlin's "poetological" reflections could ever emerge in their particular form. Indeed, as his later essays show, the general problematic of politics, religion, history, and all those discourses that "determine the sphere" of a poetic subject can only be grasped from a poetic point of view. However, Hölderlin was too sensitive to the surrounding debates in philosophy, theology and politics as to simply introduce his position as an apodictic and self-evident one. Rather, his "poetological" position was to emerge only by way of an extremely careful departure from the discursive practices and systematic intentions shared by the philosophy of his age. It is out of such considerations that, rather than offering an extensive interpretation of the long "poetological" essays contained in this volume, the following introductory remarks aim only at the *genesis*, that is, at the historical conditions that made Hölderlin's intellectual position possible and even necessary.

I

The dominant intellectual movements of the eighteenth century, beginning with Leibniz, can generally be said to have shifted emphasis from a static to a dynamic concept of reason. While no real rupture separates that century from the preceding one, it is nonetheless correct that intellectuals no longer "anticipate from the outset such 'reason' in the form of a closed system; the intellectual should rather permit this reason to unfold gradually, with ever increasing clarity and perfection."[3] Thus Newton's model of a progressive determination of the sensible world rather than the principles of Descartes' *Discourse on Method* becomes constitutive for the eighteenth century's paradigm of rationality. That is, rationality in general no longer unfolds as the mere transcendence of the empirical, but instead the implicit totality of the *ratio* is understood to be fundamentally contingent on its progressive integration with the realm of the sensible and particular.

This transformed paradigm of rationality finds its first comprehensive expression in the writings of Leibniz whose philosophy remains the root for virtually all intellectual movements of the century. For Leibniz, it is no longer a concept of God but one of truth which serves as the paradigm of rational cognition, and hence philosophy must proceed from an investigation of the very structure of all logical judgments (*propositiones*). Unlike the concept of God, the concept of truth *qua* logical judgment aims at recovering a common ground for the notions of unity and difference. Hence the analysis of judgments must always evince that the predicate is already implicit within the subject, functioning only as that which determines a subject: "the predicate, as a consequence, is always implicit in the subject as antecedent; and in this implicitness is what the nature of truth consists of."[4] Thus there obtains a notion of logic for which all judgments are analytic (*idem esse* = *inesse*), and for which all truth exists necessarily *a priori*. Such truth, then, becomes differentiated into necessary and contingent ones, that is, into truths of reason and truths of experience. Yet his distinction between *veritates necessariae* and *veritates contingentes* does not, therefore, relativize Leibniz's paradigm of truth as *inclusio*. Instead, it points to purely quantitative difference according to which the latter truths can merely approximate the former.[5]

Now, for Leibniz, any concept not only effects the *connexio* of subject and predicate, but it also serves to assimilate such (intrinsically contingent) *propositiones* to the higher order of necessary truths; a judgment (*propositio*) thus contains not only an ontic determination of a concrete subject, but *determinatio*, for Leibniz, also reflects the ongoing attempt to assimilate these essentially contingent truths to the order of necessary ones. This is also the reason for Leibniz's continuous development of concept of number as the privileged paradigm of any *connexio*. For the concept of number presents itself as a "metaphysical archetype" (Cassirer) inasmuch as its intrinsic structure already anticipates the totality of all possible applications to which it might lend itself.[6] Prior to its differentation into rational and irrational numbers, which essentially parallels that between the two notions of truth, the concept of number thus inaugurates the coexistence of a totality and unity without which no understanding of a given particular could ever occur. For Leibniz, an individual entity is intelligible only if included in, as well as subsumed under, a general concept. The single "monad"—the last consequence of Leibniz's earlier concept of number—remains nothing but "the universe itself seen from a particular viewpoint,"[7] and thus totality reveals itself as the potential of any individuality which is capable of being subsumed by the *ratio*. Leibniz's notion of the "concept" is mainly characterized by this task of integrating particulars; the concept (*qua connexio*) appears as the exclusive site of rationality, and through it alone can the status of the sensuous be determined within the projected system of the *ratio*.

Considered in and of itself, an intuition of the sensible was something irrational, and for rationalism, Newtonian science, and even for empiricism it was only by way of conceptual language that the implicit rationality, and thus the latent systematicity of a sensuous intuition could be unearthed and explored. To the extent that the sensuous is still not conceded any intrinsic value, the Cartesian dualism remains operative throughout the Enlightenment, whose philosophers, however, consider it a challenge rather than a solution. The conceptual inscription of an individual, sensuous intuition into the system of the *ratio* thus coincides with its erasure as individuality; the concrete intuition turns into a *function*. It is in the context of this remaining dualism that Pajanotis Kondylis, in his comprehensive account of the Enlightenment, attempts to contain the complexity of the epoch by saying that "all these currents [Rousseau, La Mettrie, Herder, Locke, Fichte, Marquis de Sade] and opposing tendencies must be understood in their unity, namely, as possible answers to the fundamental question, posed positively or negatively, concerning the rehabilitation of the sensuous."[8]

Yet the rationalist understanding that a sensuous intuition be valid only to the extent that it could be determined as being concurrent with the assumed systematicity of the universe was persistently challenged from its very beginnings. A noticeable, though diverse group of intellectuals, thinkers without a "system," incessantly seeks to recast the fundamental questions of cognition in a way that would not necessitate the obliteration of the individual, of the sensuous, of intuition proper.[9] In England, such reflections can be traced to the Cambridge Platonists of the preceding century, and the tradition may be said to culminate in the philosophy of Shaftesbury whose influence in Germany exceeded that of any other foreign thinker, with the possible exception of Rousseau. It is in this Neo-Platonic movement, which toward the end of the 18th century—with the philosophy of Schelling as the most prominent case in point—also involves the (clearly biased) rediscovery of the philosophy of Spinoza, that one can locate the significant intellectual positions which also characterize the theoretical writings of Hölderlin.

A first attempt to rehabilitate the sensuous, unmediated (poetic) intuition for the *ratio* was made by the Wolff disciple Alexander G. Baumgarten (1714–1762).[10] As Baumgarten's conception of the aesthetic representation as an *analogon rationis* evinces, rationality and logic as such are not put into question. Rather the notion of an individual, sensous intuition is systematically radicalized, to a point where it is considered capable of coexisting as an analogue of the *ratio*. Such a rehabilitation of the sensuous as an analogy persists through Kant whose critical philosophy not only maintains the doctrine of the essential incompatibility of the sensuous and the intelligible but is called forth precisely because such a hiatus characterizes all experience in the first place. Ideas, for Kant, have a purely regulative function, since no intuition can ever match the necessity which we must accord them *a priori*. The only suggestion at a union of the two realms occurs, as is well known, in Kant's *Critique of Judgment*. Yet not only does the notion of *intuition* oscillate for the aesthetic reflective judgment between one of reception and production, but its relation to the *ratio* is also necessarily bracketed by Kant as occurring "always according to analogical laws." As a result, we learn that no concept can ever correspond to the aesthetic reflective judgment. From the Scholastic distinction between an *ens creatum* and an *ens increatum*, to Leibniz's division between the different *veritates* and, finally, to Kant's aesthetic reflective judgment, intuition and *ratio* with their attendant semiologies of image and concept remain compatible only in the strictly virtual sense of an *analogia*.[11]

Such a problematic reconciliation of intellect and intuition was essentially preprogrammed in Leibniz's "prestabilized" yet forever deferred "harmony." Hence Alfred Bäumler seems right when observing that "because even as a critical philosopher, Kant still knew the system of harmony behind him (. . .) [his work] was not the destruction but the perfection of Leibnizianism."[12] The general dilemma of the *ratio* as the exclusive site of truth consists in the problem of matching its conceptual clarity and distinctness with an adequate intuition. Within the horizon of *ratio*, thinking was to unfold only as the analysis and dissection of individual sensuous intuition. To partake of the system of the *ratio*, an intuition had to be converted into a function, conceptualized and thus made to surrender its individuality. For the philosophy of Enlightenment, intellect and intuition remain fundamentally irreconcilable.

While the conception of sensuous intuition as an *analogon rationis* only restored the intuition to rationality, but did not outrightly contest the validity of the assumed hiatus separating one from the other, the second half of the eighteenth century witnessed a radicalization of this problem. The gradual decay of Wolff's popular philosophy, the increasing impact of Pietism, a Protestant movement that grew particularly strong in Hölderlin's native Swabia, and finally the significant impact of Shaftesbury's philosophy all contributed to the peculiar reinterpretation of Leibniz and Spinoza throughout the second half of the century. The anti-dogmatic, anti-theological tendency of German Pietism aimed essentially at restoring an immediacy of intuition to religious experience, and its representatives were mostly concerned with securing for intuition a self-sufficient status and independence from the intellect as the mediating faculty. Hence a notion like that of "inwardness" (*Innigkeit*), which holds operative function in Hölderlin's later essays, still echoes the considerable influence of Pietism on his intellectual position.[13]

In addition to the still considerable influence of Pietism, it is also the philosophy of Shaftesbury which contributes to a specific reinterpretation of Leibniz's work, now directed toward an ultimate convergence of intuition and the supersensuous. This reinterpretation involves the dismissal of Leibniz's disjunction of the intellect and the sensuous while simultaneously stressing his notion of a teleological union of the two.[14] In clear adherence to its Platonic origins, this historical movement of the later 18th Century unfolds predominantly around the notion of "love" (eros). The Platonism of this anti-rationalist current, which is particularly evident in the work of Shaftsbury, Hemsterhuis and Herder, also remains the dominant intellectual feature of Hölderlin's early letters.[15]

II

In his *Symposium* and in the "Phaedrus" Plato introduces eros as a force eternally striving to grasp the "whole," though forever failing to accomplish this goal. The concrete realm in which eros becomes manifest is that of beauty, the "aesthetic." One of the first to discuss the concept of eros not as a psychological "disposition" of a given subject, but as something which exceeds and axiologically precedes psychological theories of the subject, is Frans Hemsterhuis (1721–1790). In his "Lettre sur les Désirs." Hemsterhuis states that "the desire of the soul is a tendency toward the perfect and intimate union with the essence of the desired object."[16] While friendship (amitié) is still grounded in our mutual relation to an "altogether particular object" ("une chose qui nous est tout-à-fait particulière"), love exceeds these rational boundaries of mere object-determinedness.

> In truth, all that which is visible or sensible for us tends toward unity or union. However, everything is composed of absolutely isolated individuals; and that beautiful appearance of a fittingly connected chain of beings notwithstanding, it seems clear that

each individual exists to exist and not for the existence of an other.[17]

In contrast to rationalist philosophy which, as "speculative psychology" (Wolff), seeks to determine the subject and its desires exclusively as a set of attitudes toward concrete beings, love is here no longer defined via its object but—by determining the very structure of existence as such—forms the condition of possibility for any such psychology in the first place. Even though Hemsterhuis ultimately remains within the rationalist framework of the sensible/intelligible dualism, his conception of the *eros* as a force with ontological implications pushes Descartes' dualism again beyond Wolff's more limited epistemological framework. A primordial unity of things reappears negatively in our eternal and unfulfilled striving to reestablish it.[18] In a clearly Platonic turn, the very idea of such a primordial unity is interpreted as evidence that rational thinking is grounded in a unity which precedes, and hence remains inaccessible to, its conceptual and analytical disjunctions.

A translation of Hemsterhuis' essay by J. G. Herder appeared in 1781 together with a critical commentary by Herder entitled "Love and Selfhood" (*Liebe und Selbstheit*).[19] Against Hemsterhuis, for whose ideas he otherwise offers great praise, Herder argues that friendship rather than the *eros* is apt to effect this union. For unlike love, friendship preserves the individuality of its partners, and it can thus only be matched by parental love. Yet the stakes remain essentially unchanged and it is specifically in Hölderlin's early letters that we first notice the extent to which extent this Neo-Platonist rethinking of the *ratio* influenced his thinking. In a letter to his friend Neuffer from July 1793 (No. 60), Hölderlin gives a fictitious account of how, "resting among the disciples of Plato," he would follow the movement of a "magnificent [power] into the utmost depth, to the remotest regions of the land of spirit, where the soul of the world emanates its life into the thousand pulses of nature, whereto the effluvious forces return in their immeasurable circle." The letter continues:

> Intoxicated by the Socratic chalice and by Socratic friendship, I would listen at the meal to the enchanted youths as they

would pay tribute to the sacred love with tender, fiery speech
(. . .) and, finally, how the master, the divine Socrates himself
with his heavenly wisdom would teach them all what love is, . . .

However, Hölderlin's conception of "love" is not to be
understood as an unproblematic and, as it were, mystical inroad
to the primordial "depth" and unity of all Being. Rather, Hölderlin conceives of the *eros* as only one of this unity's two principles, and the far-reaching ambitions of the *eros* continue to
obscure the ground itself. As Gerhard Kurz and Dieter Henrich
have shown, *Hyperion* restates this problem as with its image of
an "excentric path," a movement through time without a coor-
dinating center.[20] Following this letter, Hölderlin repeatedly and
with increasing philosophical rigor returns to this problem of a
primordial union. It is particularly in his initial exploration of
the Neo-Platonist project of overcoming the sensible/intelligible
dualism without relegating the concrete, individual intuition to
a merely ancillary *function*, that Hölderlin develops a profound
interest in Kant's critical philosophy—particularly in his *Critique
of Judgment*—as well as in the theoretical writings of Schiller.

When considered within the context of the strong anti-
rationalist current in the 18th century, with its rehabilitation of
eros as an existential principle and the aesthetic as a realm no
longer inferior to that of rationality and logic,[21] the advent of
Kant's critical philosophy proves a more complex event than the
mere twilight of empiricism and rationalist psychology. Most of
Hölderlin's reception of Kant occurs during his education at the
seminary at Tübingen, a period marked by increasing intellectual
surveillance and repression on part of the ruling duke who fears
that the French Revolution might inspire similar unrest on his
territory. During these earlier years of the Revolution, Hölderlin
and his friends, among them Hegel and Schelling, are avidly
reading Plato, Spinoza, Lessing, Jacobi, Rousseau and—Kant.
The tradition of a Plato-inspired anti-intellectualism which Swabian Pietism unsuccessfully sought to manipulate for its own,
rather narrow-minded, interests, characterizes the reception of
Kant in the Tübingen seminary even more than the great rationalist and empiricist "systems" of Leibniz and of German *Schul-
metaphysik.*[22] Thus the young Hegel devotes much of his time in

Tübingen and Bern to a thorough study of Kant and the question of his "applicability." Specifically Hegel's early writings constitute such an attempt to reconcile Kant's critical pilosophy with the Neo-Platonists' demand for a primordial union of the sensible and intelligible. As a result, the Platonic notion of the *eros* continues to hold a central position in Hegel's "Positivity of Christian Religion" and in "The Spirit of Christianity and its Fate."[23]

Neither too young already to move beyond Kant, as was Schelling, nor too isolated from the post-Kantian development in philosophy, as was Hegel in Bern, Hölderlin was in a position to think with Kant and yet have access to a critical perspective on his critical philosophy. Hölderlin's first explorations of the possibility of a primordial union must be understood in their genesis out of Kant's and Fichte's "critical idealism." Ostensibly, Hölderlin's early theoretical writings continue to pose their questions within the conceptual boundaries defined by specifically these two philosophers, and the question of an ontological, unified substratum underlying all phenomena of the sensible and intelligible is initially posed as a theoretical, philosophical one. Beginning around Summer 1793, (cf. letter to Neuffer, No. 60) until roughly Spring 1796 (cf. letter to Niethammer No. 117), Hölderlin devotes much of his reflection to a theoretical formulation and solution of this Neo-Platonic problem: as shall be seen, his answer proves doubly sceptical. For in the process of his exploration of the general problematic of a primordial union, Hölderlin not only realizes the impossibility of such an undertaking, but also recognizes the theoretical and philosophical as the very condition for this impossibility. As we observed before, the Platonic conception of the *eros*, for Hölderlin, constitutes but one dimension in what is an essentially "excentric" movement through time. Thus it comes as no surprise that Hölderlin's notion of "beauty" also differs from Platonic and Neo-Platonic thinkers such as Hemsterhuis, Shaftesbury and Herder, who generally consider it the outward manifestation of the very unity intended by the *eros*.

Realizing that philosophy's dependency on the category of difference necessarily prevents an "intuition" of the primordial ground of Being, Hölderlin eventually recasts the function of the aesthetic as such. Due to the inescapable "excentricity" of all reflection, the aesthetic can no longer be considered a mere function of a theoretical, rationalist system. As the following examination of Hölderlin's early essays is meant to show, Hölderlin's later texts, the so-called "Homburg writings," should thus not be read as an aesthetic theory remaining essentially subordinate and subservient to the philosophical (Hegel), nor as a privileged mode of presentation such as affords philosophy its own, systematic completion (Schelling). On the contrary, it is out of a specific insight into a fundamental aporia of philosophical discourse that Hölderlin develops his complex and seemingly idiosyncratic "doctrine of the alternation of tones." As remains to be shown, this doctrine should not be read as a somewhat peculiar "theory of art" within the broader context of German Idealist aesthetics but as a "poetology" which, to some extent, represents a commentary on the intrinsic problematics of any philosophical aesthetics.

III

Hölderlin's first three essays, entitled "On the Law of Freedom," "On the Concept of Punishment," and "Judgment and Being" were all written around Winter 1794–95. By the time he moves from Waltershausen to Jena in order to assume his position as tutor at the von Kalb family, Hölderlin has just read Schiller's influential essay *Über Anmuth und Würde*, ("On Grace and Dignity"), Plato's *Phaedrus* and Kant's *Critique of Judgment.*[24] As Hölderlin states in a letter to Neuffer, he plans to write "an essay about the *aesthetic* ideas" that can be considered "a commentary of Plato's *Phaedrus.*" The main interest, so his letter continues, is the "analysis of the beautiful and the sublime, according to which the Kantian philosophy is simplified, [yet], on the other hand, rendered more manifold, as Schiller has partially already done it in his essay *Anmuth und Würde.*" However, Hölderlin immediately adds, Schiller "risked a step too little beyond the Kantian threshold than, in my opinion, he should have risked."[25]

Yet the subsequent letter, in which Hölderlin reports his first impressions about his stay at Jena to his friend Neuffer, reveals that this "step beyond the Kantian threshold" had already been taken, namely, by Fichte.[26] While attending Fichte's classes and studying his works, Hölderlin struggles to understand the implications of Fichte's steps beyond Kant. It is because of this sudden development of Hölderlin's philosophical interest, that the three fragments, which date from November 1794 to the first half of 1795, have to be read as inextricably interwoven with what turned out to be the point of transition from critical philosophy to dialectics.[27] As an engaged student of this transformation, Hölderlin begins to develop, at first more in the form of a commentary on certain concepts, some very unusual ideas which this "turn" toward Idealism seems to imply for the realm of the aesthetic.

> There is a natural state of the imagination which has in common the lawlessness with that anarchy of representations organized by the intellect, to be sure, yet which, with respect to the law by which it is to be organized, needs to be distinguished from intellect.
>   By this natural state of imagination, by this lawlessness, I mean a moral one; by this law, [I mean] the law of freedom.
>   There, the imagination is considered in and of itself, here in conjunction with the faculty of desire.

This opening passage from Hölderlin's essay "On the Law of Freedom," sets forth the distinction between an "anarchy of representations" and a "natural state of imagination" and parallels it with that between "intellect" and "the law of freedom." The latter two are meant to compensate for a disorder implied by the former ones. As the last sentence shows, the imagination is at stake in either situation, once being considered "in and of itself," while the other time in relation to the "faculty of desire." It is apparent that the distinctions made thus far reflect on a somewhat general level those in Kant's first and second *Critiques*; while the former work explores the theoretical realm, namely, our understanding of natural causality, the *Second Critique* addresses the practical domain of Reason, which involves the causality of freedom as it emerges from the "faculty of desire" (*Begehrungsvermögen*). Hölderlin continues by elaborating the two distinctions that he has proposed thus far:

> In that anarchy of representations where the imagination is
> considered theoretically, a unity of the manifold, an ordering
> of perceptions was indeed possible yet accidental.
> In this natural state of fantasy where it [the imagination] is
> considered in relation to the faculty of desire, moral lawfulness
> is indeed possible yet accidental.

Although Hölderlin will subsequently not focus on the theoretical aspect of the imagination, that is, on questions addressed
by Kant's *Critique of Pure Reason*, it is important to notice how
he conceives of the realm of the theoretical as such. Whereas
Kant's theory of knowledge (assuming that the First *Critique* is,
to some extent, a work about epistemology) deals only with
necessary conditions of possibility for synthetic judgments, Hölderlin recasts the realm of the theoretical as susceptible to contingency. The "ordering of perceptions," he writes, is "possible
yet accidental." The somewhat open structure of the sentence
in question leaves it undecided what role the imagination holds
in the allegedly random occurrence of such a "synthesis." However, Hölderlin's argument that the realm of the theoretical is
not necessarily coherent is an obvious disagreement with Kant.
It already implies that the very systematicity and coherence which
transcendental philosophy proclaims for itself still needs to be
grounded.

It is striking how Hölderlin's seemingly idiosyncratic assessment of the function of the imagination in Kant's First *Critique*
points to the indeed crucial problem of how to secure the realm
of the transcendental as an a priori coherent and systematic one.[28]
By conceiving of this realm as contingent on the "accidental"
workings of the imagination, Hölderlin implicitly reveals something about the general thrust of his philosophical interest.
Namely, the reliance of the transcendental, which is the veritable
realm of philosophy, on what Kant calls the "transcendental
imagination" is problematic, since that faculty precedes axiologically that which it grounds. Being assigned such an ontolog-
ically prior status, that is, a place extrinsic to the realm which
it shall ground, the imagination implicitly threatens the alleged
systematicity of the theoretical as such. While the historical
development of Kant's system involves the eventual relegation
of the imagination to a merely reproductive and hence derivative

function, it is also true that the very idea of that unity which a specific synthetic judgment merely *applies* to a given intuition cannot itself be grounded theoretically.[29] The origins of Kant's presupposed transcendental synthesis, on which the synthesizing intellect always already relies, cannot be traced, and the very possibility of such a synthesis must, at least for the time being, be considered "accidental."

However, as the continuation of the fragment evinces, Hölderlin is less interested in this theoretical aspect of the imagination than in its relation to the faculty of desire. The realm of that relation is characterized as "fantasy." Once again, the "moral lawfulness," which is the objective of the faculty of desire and whose unity is preformed by the imagination that collaborates with it, remains "possible yet accidental."

> There is an aspect of the empirical faculty of desire, the analogue of what is called nature, which is most prominent where necessity and freedom, the restricted and the unrestricted, the sensuous and the sacred seem to unite; a natural innocence or, one might say, a morality of the instinct; and the fantasy in tune with it is heavenly.

According to Kant, this "aspect of the empirical faculty of desire, the analogue of what is called nature" becomes intuitable precisely within the realm of art.[30] Thus far, then, there seems little reason to consider Hölderlin's argument more than a somewhat idiosyncratic tracing of the main systematic positions of Kant's critical philosophy. Hölderlin's notion of a "natural innocence," too, appears as but an echo of Kant's concept of *Genius*. However, when speaking of the "analogue of what is called nature," Hölderlin does *not* refer to it as art. Nor can it be argued that its subjective import is limited to the pre-conceptual conformity of an intuition and the intellect, as Kant had developed it in his theory of the aesthetic, reflective judgment. By ascribing this "analogue" as an "aspect" to the faculty of desire, Hölderlin could, at best, be understood to approximate Kant's notion of a teleological judgment.[31] For, as he argues, this "aspect" is phenomenally most prominent where "necessity and *freedom* seem to unite." Hölderlin's almost instantaneous paraphrase of the

Kantian opposition between "freedom and necessity" with the distinction between the "sensuous and the sacred" suggests that the union which he wishes to point to occurs *directly* within the subject and is not bracketed as an analogical or hypothetical construct. In this sense, a union between "sensuous and the sacred" remains discontinuous with Kant's view that the concept of practical Reason, freedom, is fundamentally incommensurable with the realm of the sensuous and of intuition.[32]

The "law of freedom" delineates the convergence of *ratio* and intuition as they establish the concept of freedom within subjectivity itself. Whereas for Kant no intuition can correspond to the a priori certain idea of freedom—concepts of reason are by definition non-intuitable for Kant—unless in the form of a symbolic *analogon*, Hölderlin's intuition seeks to overcome the realm of analogy as the definitive boundary of critical philosophy. Namely, Hölderlin recasts the convergence of "freedom and necessity" as the most primordial synthesis of intellect and intuition itself, a synthesis which takes place within the subject itself. He thus approaches what Kant had repeatedly ruled out as an "intellectual intuition." According to Kant, no intuition could ever function as the *ratio cognoscendi* for the concept of freedom.[33] However, Hölderlin does not simply stabilize this convergence of intuition and the intelligible in an ontological sense either; for its occurrence, linked to the creative imagination, is "accidental," that is, it cannot be theoretically grounded as a necessity. Consequently Hölderlin concedes that "it is a mere fortune to be thus attuned." The "law of freedom," then, becomes manifest only through a contingent causality. The remainder of the fragment, as well as the subsequent essay, entitled "On the Concept of Punishment," will elaborate on the nature of precisely that causality.

"The first time the law of freedom discloses itself to us, it appears as punishing," Hölderlin says, and he continues: "The origin of all our virtue occurs in evil. Thus morality can never be entrusted to nature." As is well known, such a position dates back at least as far as Rousseau and indeed, based on Rousseau's *Contrat Social*, Kant himself had developed virtually the same argument.[34] However, Hölderlin affords this position a rather striking reinterpretation. For, according to his statements, the seeming union of "freedom and necessity," of the "sensuous and the sacred" can occur only analeptically. The primordial ground of their shared origin becomes phenomenally manifest only after a transgression, "a moral lawlessness" has occurred. Thus the "anarchy of representations" which characterizes the realm of fantasy cannot be overcome by taking recourse to a pre-existing conception of unity. The idea of unity, that is, of a latent systematicity of the transcendental realm remains accidental, more specifically, it is contingent on the experience of punishment. Only after some form of punishment has occurred, is it possible to trace the "law of morality" which might overcome the prevailing "anarchy of representations."

Hölderlin essentially seeks to inquire into the primordial unity from which the division between a natural and a rational causality must have originated. With the concept of punishment as a *ratio cognoscendi* of a primordeal order where "freedom and necessity" seem to have converged, Hölderlin implicitly introduces a temporal marker into Kant's conceptual system. For only an analeptic "intellectual intuition" which follows such punishment, permits the mediation of what Kant, in his *Critique of Judgment*, still seeks to evince as compatible through the non-temporal *analogon* of art. According to Hölderlin's argumentation, the primordial ground of any philosophy becomes accessible only by way of a contingency. Hölderlin's notion of an "intellectual intuition," a quasi Platonic *anamnesis*, brought about by what he refers to as punishment, that is, by something "accidental," thus raises the question concerning the very possibility of a *prima philosophia* as "non-excentric."

In continuation of the problems that Hölderlin's raises in his first essay, the subsequent fragment, "On the Concept of Punishment," now focuses on the very recognizability of punishment *as* punishment. Dating around January/February 1795, the fragmentary text reflects the increasing influence of Fichte's early philosophy in that Hölderlin situates an essentially epistemological problem, the recognizability of the moral law, within the general horizon of ethics. After rejecting, very much in accordance with Kant, an empirical approach to this question, Hölderlin goes on to show how "the moral law announces itself negatively and, as something infinite, cannot announce itself differently." However, it appears that the shift from the empirical to the transcendental, that is, to an internal order of evidence, still does not resolve the problem. For the law of morality, the "immediate voice in us" of the Kantian and Fichtean "ought," still discloses itself only by default as "a result of the fact that we willed something which is opposed to the law of morality." As Hölderlin argues, the mere reliance on the law's *resistance* as its *ratio cognoscendi* would lead to the fatalistic conclusion that "all suffering [of resistance] is punishment."

Indeed it appears that the distinction between a "cause of cognition" and a "real cause" remains itself insufficient for tracing the origins of punishment itself. [35]

> Still, the distinction between a cause of cognition and a real cause seems to be of little help. If the resistance of the law against my will is punishment, and if I recognize the law only with the punishment, the question arises: can I recognize the law through the punishment? and then: can I be punished for transgressing a law that I was not aware of?

It would be reductive to interpret the ethical terminology prevailing in the first two essays as evidence that Hölderlin is adressing only concrete ethical issues. For, as the very problematic raised in this paragraph shows, the question of epistemology is already enclosed by the general horizon of ethics. Thus to raise the question concerning the recognizability of the moral law *as* law encloses that concerning the very possibility of philosophical systematicity and order on which all epistemology is always already based. Toward the end of the fragment, Hölderlin attempts to tell apart punishment from mere suffering by stating that, "insofar as one considers oneself punished, one necessarily implies the transgression of the law within oneself."[36] The Platonic logic— considering the *idea* of punishment as evidence for the "existence of a moral law within oneself"—illustrates Hölderlin's reconception of the paradigm of order as such. Order, the essential premise for any philosophical systematicity whatsoever, is no longer conceived of as a necessary correlate of the manifold grounding in what Kant called "transcendental apperception," but as a dialectical movement which unfolds within subjectivity itself. As a result, Hölderlin's reassessment of a primordial and unitary ground of all Being as an analeptic (quasi Platonic) *anamnesis*, poses a serious challenge to the possibility of an integral subjectivity, that is, to the continuity of a "self" as such.[37]

Hölderlin's thesis that a primordial order and unity can only be grasped a posteriori, when instigated by punishment, must not be discarded as a fatalistic or merely idiosyncratic philosophical position that ought to be overcome. On the contrary, Hölderlin recognizes the profound implication of this thesis, that the *aporia*, the intrinsic temporal hiatus which punishment introduces into consciousness, cannot be overcome once again within the discursive boundaries of either transcendental or practical philosophy. In this sense, Friedrich Strack's interpretation of the two early Hölderlin essays remains unsatisfactory when he proposes a reconciliation of the law of morality and the law of freedom by way of education.[38] With the concept of education, one would simply abandon the realm of the transcendental for that of the empirical. Thus Strack conflates "coercion" and "punishment." However, the concept of "coercion" as a means of education implies the manipulation of an already existing positive order, whereas "punishment," as discussed by Hölderlin, is veritably constitutive of our *knowledge* of such an order in the first place. Thus Hölderlin writes in a letter to his brother that "what happens due to coercion is not the act of a good will" and therefore does not "approximate the highest law."[39]

It is in his essay "Judgment and Being," the last of his early philosophical fragments, that Hölderlin addresses the question of a systematic *prima philosophia* most thoroughly. Through a formal analysis of "judgment," in the sense of Leibniz's *propositio*, Hölderlin seeks to determine to what extent man's intellect has ever access to Being as an integral and yet completely determined totality. The first section, possibly a text independent from the rest (the title is Beissner's),[40] reads:

> *Judgment.* in the highest and strictest sense, is the original separation of object and subject which are most deeply united in intellectual intuition, that separation through which alone object and subject become possible, the arche-separation. In the concept of separation, there lies already the concept of

the reciprocity of object and subject and the necessary presupposition of a whole of which object and subject form the
parts. "I am I" is the most fitting example for this concept of
arche-separation, for in the practical arche-separation "I"
opposes the *non-I, not itself.*

The two conceptions of judgment introduced here are both
clearly Fichtean. The first and (as the last two paragraphs evidence) for Hölderlin more crucial one is the proposition "I am
I." It is, as Hölderlin says, "the most fitting example" of a "theoretical" judgment. By judgment Hölderlin understands the most
primordial separation (cf. the German *Ur-teil*), that one which
rends apart for the first time the "necessary presupposition of a
whole of which object and subject form the parts." Here Hölderlin follows Fichte's *Science of Knowledge* which takes this judgment for its starting point.[41] The "I = I" proposition is the "Act"
(*Tathandlung*) which allows the *Science* to unfold as system; it is
not meant as a tautological identification of "I" and "I," nor does
it outrightly posit the "I" as a reified subject or consciousness.[42]
Rather, such an "Act" seeks to establish the primordial order
which permits Fichte's "reflection of the absolute subject" to
unfold as a coherent and systematic one. The Fichtean "Act"
posits neither an ontological substratum, a reified absolute subjectivity, and even less a concrete consciousness; rather, it inaugurates an order within which such concretizations are always
already formally grounded. In his discussion of this fundamental
notion of the "Act"—the veritable basis for Fichte's conception
of knowledge—Ernst Cassirer observes:

> The positing of the 'A' identical with itself implies the self-
> certainty of the grounding relation throughout the multiplicity
> of all possible moments and applications wherein the cognition
> of the A constitutes itself. That a certain content "is" identical
> with itself means that it is as such *recognizable*: and this rec-
> ognition can never be achieved by a mere "perception" but
> only by an intuition which encompasses the infinity and total-
> ity of all possible perceptions.[43]

Fichte's proposition of identity posits a "theoretical" order
which proleptically encompasses all possible determinations of

its constituents; in this sense, the Fichtean "Act" identifies no substances but inaugurates an ontological unity which allows for the progressive systematization and determination of its concrete differentials. Writing his remarks as a close reader of Fichte's *Science of Knowledge* and as a student in Fichte's 1794–95 lectures in Jena, Hölderlin realizes that such a formal postulate requires a practical counterpart. Thus he speaks of a "practical arche-separation" where the "'I' opposes *the non-I*," a notion which, once again echoes Fichte's concept of the "reciprocal determination" of "I" and "non-I." The conception of a "whole" in terms of an "I" and a "non-I", of a posited reality and its negation, already indicates that the "I" is not to be understood as a positive consciousness. Rather, the "reciprocal determination" (*Wechselbestimmung*) represents the formal matrix within which consciousness arrives at knowledge. "The 'I' in question is not an isolated or isolable part of Being; it is in this sense not mere 'subjectivity' but the primordeal identity of the subjective and objective."[44] Likewise, Hölderlin speaks of the "reciprocity" of subject and object.

However, despite his close adherence to Fichte's operative terminology, it is important to note that Hölderlin emphasizes the aspect of *separation* as the one most relevant for judgment. The Fichtean "Act" and the "reciprocal determination" thus appear as correlates of an already fallen and ultimately derivative structure. For if the first of the two notions creates the totality of an order and the second, complementary one, assures that the order be "determined," then Being, an always progressing and negating correlate of "I" and "non-I" can only be grasped as *difference*. Difference, for Fichte, is the absolute *sine qua non* of philosophy, for which reason Fichte sees an absolute unity not as the origin but as the telos of all knowledge; by extension, "thinking" in the *Science* is systematic precisely to the extent that it is reflexive, able to double back on its object. Thus reflexivity determines both, the concrete differentials of the "system" as well as this system itself in relation to its telos of an ultimate unity. In this sense, Fichte's notion of Being must be understood as an *ought* that impels the "reciprocal determination" of "I" and "non-I" and thus determines the totality of all difference.[45] Rather than designating a primordial coherence, an absolute substance or subjectivity, Fichte's concept of Being is to be understood as the predicate of coherence and systematicity conferred upon a structure which can only match those attributes through the progressive determination of its differentials in the constant perspective of a unified telos.

The argumentation of the first two essays displays what one might call Hölderlin's "ontological skepticism," a scepticism which not only exceeds the stabilized consciousness of the Cartesian *dubito* but which—although any such claim requires the utmost caution—may even be seen to challenge the systematicity through which, as the "self-fulfilling skepticism," Hegel's phenomenological dialectic reaches its fulfilment. Hölderlin challenges the possibility of ever determining the primordial and systematic ground of Being. Thus it comes as no surprise that in "Judgment and Being" he also deviates from Fichte's conception of Being. When elaborating on the first definition of Being, the "connection between subject and object," he writes:

> Where subject and object are united altogether and not only in part, that is, united in such a manner that no separation can be performed without violating the essence of what is to be separated, there and nowhere else can be spoken of *Being proper*, as is the case with intellectual intuition.

Being is not conceived of as the coherence of a primordial "Act" which guarantees the possibility of reflexivity and the progressive reciprocal determination of the differentials of "I" and "non-I." For Hölderlin, Being is the very condition of possibility for any such reflexive separation. Whatever its "essence" may be, Being is thought to precede any synthetic unity to which the immanent reflexivity of the *Wechselbestimmung* remains confined. Thus Hölderlin continues by saying that "this Being must not be confused with identity." For him, the totality implied by the Fichtean "Act," the proposition "I = I," is already a derivative one, since it does not examine the implicit separation that accompanies any notion of "I" as such.

> How can I say : "I" without self-consciousness? Yet how is self-consciousness possible? In opposing myself to myself, separating myself from myself, yet in recognizing myself as the same

in the opposed regardless of this separation. Yet to what extent
as the same? I can, I must ask in this manner; for in another
respect it [the "I"] is opposed to itself. Hence identity is not
a union of object and subject which simply occured, hence
identity is not = to absolute Being.

At the cost of reifying Fichte's notion of the "I," a misconception which he shares with some of today's interpreters of
Fichte, and which his letter to Hegel displays even more clearly,[46]
Hölderlin shows how Being can neither be conceived of as an
identity nor as a synthesis. Likewise, Being does not coincide
with the transcendental category of the absolute "I" either, since
any transcendentalism also implies, on the part of the intellect,
a separation from that which it transcends. It appears that by
showing how all notions of reflexivity, synthesis and identity are
already derivatives of the "presupposition of a whole," Hölderlin
has disqualified transcendental philosophy as such from any participation in what he understands by Being. The question thus
arises of how Being can ever become manifest. More specifically,
the question concerning the phenomenality of Being might be
rephrased to ask what Hölderlin's "intellectual intuition" is an
intuition of: What does Hölderlin understand by an "intellectual
intutition"?

Before exploring any further Hölderlin's particular notion
of an "intellectual intuition," it may be helpful to briefly recall
its historical origins. Since such an "intellectual intuition" was
always understood as being bound up with a conception of a
totality, it is crucial to keep it distinct from Kant's notion of
Anschauung, which is essentially an unstructured, sensuous appre-
hension.[47] Yet neither does such an "intuition" partake of any
conceptual and discursive order, such as would appear to be the
foundation of all modern philosophical systems. Historically, it
is already with the desubstantialization of the concept of God in
the work of Nicholas of Cues, that the idea of what he calls a
visio intellectualis becomes a possible and indeed necessary form
of cognition for man.[48] Namely, Cues transposes the notion of
infinitude from the object of cognition (God) onto the process
of cognition itself. Far from any claims for the possibility of an
absolute cognition, Cues nevertheless realizes that—intellectual

limitations (*docta ignorantia*) notwithstanding—man requires a direction for his intellectual efforts. Hence Aquinas' *Scientia Dei* is interpreted by Cues as a genitivus objectivus, as a telos which requires that we locate infinitude within the process of cognition itself. "Until we have not obtained knowledge of Him, the spirit will not come to rest."[49] With Nicholas of Cues, then, the intellect is recognized to be in need of a "sense" of totality, however virtual, without which both its sensuous and discursive actions would remain without meaning and orientation.

It is once again with Leibniz, that this notion of a *visio* is assimilated to concerns of rationalist philosophy. For Leibniz and an "intuitive cognition" (*cognitio intuitiva*) becomes the culminating point for his hierarchy of cognitions. As we already saw, Leibniz seeks to determine the scope of knowledge through a formal analysis of judgments, and in the course of his analysis it was the notion of an *inclusio* of the predicate within the subject which validated the judgment itself (*inesse = idem esse*). Now, in order to secure the identity of subject and predicate as a veritable one, it is necessary to *determine* our cognitions completely with respect to their distinct features (*requisita*).[50] Cognitions which have been fully determined, Leibniz refers to as adequate. Although sceptical about man's capacity of arriving at such cognitions,[51] Leibniz here already summarizes all the central criteria for what Fichte, Schelling and—although with marked differences—Hölderlin bring to bear on an "intellectual intuition." "And because a notion is often composite, we cannot simultaneously have knowledge of all criteria for these notions: however, where such is possible, or where the leap into the whole is possible, I call the cognition intuitive."[52] Only a non-representational cognition is capable of totality, namely, because it is not bound up with some symbolic order and thus temporalized. Such a completely determined totality, Leibniz calls God (*ens perfectissimum*), and the ideas, though imperfect, bear witness to his/its existence.[53] For post-Leibnizian philosophy, this idea coincides almost entirely with the notion of reason (*Vernunft*).

In addition to discussing the abstract problematic of a philosophical ontology through the category of an intellectual intuition, Hölderlin also introduces this concept in his later "poetological" writings as characteristic of the "tragic." "The tragic poem," he writes, "is the metaphor of an intellectual intuition." Hölderlin's transference of the conception of an "intellectual intuition" from the abstract issues at stake in his early fragments onto the "tragic poem" underscores the fundamental continuity between his philosophical and poetical concerns. Apart from the fragments discussed here, the earlier Hölderlin also elaborates his notion of "intellectual intuition" in two central letters to Schiller and Niethammer (No. 104 and 117). Again, it is Fichte whose use of this concept is decisive for our understanding of its function within the text of Hölderlin. Although the most explicit statements by Fichte on "intellectual intuition" are to be found in his "Second Introduction" to the *Science of Knowledge* from 1797, it is legitimate to say that he merely elaborates what his review of the Kant critic "Aenesidemus" had already implied.[54] As Fichte puts it at one point quite unambiguously, "intellectual intuition is the only firm standpoint for philosophy."[55] It "occurs at every moment of consciousness," and thus it is already marked as a correlate of the very progression of the *Science* as well as the principle assuring the coherence and systematicity of that progression.[56] Hence Fichte remarks that "the philosopher thereby discovers this intellectual intuition as a fact for consciousness (for him it is a fact; for the original self an act)."[57] However, Fichte's conception of "intellectual intuition" not only involves the progressive and reciprocal determination of the "I" and "non-I" as an "Act," but—as the intuition of the totality of all possible determinations—it simultaneously determines this "reciprocal determination" from the perspective of its ultimate telos. For Fichte, "intellectual intuition" is at once the condition of possibility for the "Act" and the guarantee of its ultimate determination, thus assuring that the individual and reciprocal determinations are not random, or "accidental" as Hölderlin would say, but that they are integrated into the intuition of the absolute "I" as a "fact."

Yet in displacing Fichte's absolute "I" by aligning it with a finite, individuated notion of consciousness, Hölderlin does not invest Being or the intelligible with an absolute systematicity from the outset. On the contrary, within the discursive and temporal boundaries of systematic philosophical thinking, Being can only be grasped at the cost of our violating its "essence." As demonstrated in the last paragraph of Hölderlin's fragment, this violation occurs at the very moment that a subject asserts its individuality and has already performed this violation—"how can I say: 'I' without self-consciousness (. . .) separating myself from myself." The transgression, the shattering of the essence of Being, is inescapable; for, as Hölderlin's previous essays argue, it is only through punishment that the "moral law" announces itself. The glance at Being afforded by an intellectual intuition is always only one of analepse. Thus Nicholas' of Cues *visio intellectualis* no longer assures man's *scientia Dei* of its meaning and coherence; instead, it involves man's recognition that, being irreducably bound up with a symbolic order and its attendant temporality, he can only have a more or less developed awareness of the impossibility of recuperating the withdrawn God without, once again, shattering his creation.

IV

The three fragments from Jena represent Hölderlin's encounter with the emerging philosophy of German Idealism, and thus his early writings have been read, with varying emphases and results, as a major contribution to the development of dialectics. Beginning with Ernst Cassirer's essay "Hölderlin und der deutsche Idealismus," a number of Hölderlin's interpreters—Wilhelm Böhm, Johannes Hoffmeister, Ernst Müller, among others—display a tendency to credit Hölderlin with having made a significant contribution to the development of Hegel's and Schelling's dialectics. While this thesis has only recently received its most forceful expression by Pajanotis Kondylis (*Die Entstehung der Dialektik*) it seems necessary to point out that Hölderlin himself developed a markedly different position in his later writings. Interpreters of Hölderlin's theoretical enterprise have largely failed to assess its scope other than as a prolegomenon to the great systems of German Idealism. Yet as already the analysis of his early fragments revealed, Hölderlin's indisputable influence on Schelling and Hegel does not reflect his own theoretical concerns, precisely because he conceives of the theoretical itself as an activity which can only gloss over or acknowledge the lack of its proper foundation. In this regard, Schelling's integration of the concept of "intellectual intuition" with the aesthetic remains markedly different from Hölderlin's understanding of this concept. For to the extent that Schelling views the aesthetic as the phenomenal and "objective" quality of such an intuition, thus providing closure for his *System of Transcendental Idealism*, he reinstates it as a grounding function rather than as an intuition of the very impossibility of ever grounding a totality.[58]

In order to indicate the continuity which is intrinsic to Hölderlin's own theoretical writings, it is therefore necessary to briefly outline how the "poetological" writings of the Homburg era develop his position. If the philosophy of German Idealism can be characterized as the systematic interpretation of the *ratio* under the paradigm of an absolute and systematically accessible subjectivity,[59] Hölderlin's reflections may indeed be seen to address that same problem, yet they certainly offer an answer altogether different from that of Schelling or Hegel.

As Hölderlin's early fragments argue, an intellectual intuition of Being, that is, the intuition of a unity that antedates any structure of synthesis, identity and consciousness, must be aesthetic. Furthermore it appeared that for Hölderlin the aesthetic itself *is* not simply this intuition but can, once again, only reveal its occurrence *a posteriori*. Thus the aesthetic does not serve as the "objective" manifestation of the union between the subjective and the objective (Schelling), but only affords man an "accidental" glimpse into a past that was never quite present. For Hölderlin, then, the aesthetic manifestation of an intellectual intuition cannot occur systematically, mainly because it is the essential characteristic of such an intuition that it recognizes the impossibility of an absolute system. For only through a transgression, through the disjunction of its unity does Being veritably disclose itself. Intuition occurs only as the remembering of its ontological unity. As Else Buddeberg observes in her very lucid discussion of Hölderlin's turn to poetological concerns, "Hölderlin found a solution which, within the idealist aesthetics of his epoch, must be considered autonomous."[60] For Hölderlin, the aesthetic no longer constitutes a monumentalized *function* of a philosophical system, but instead it provides us with the tragic and elegaic recognition of the latter's impossibility. Privileging elegy and tragedy as his principal forms of poetic expression, Hölderlin can, in fact, define the "tragic poem" as "the metaphor of an intellectual intuition."

Concluding our assessment of Hölderlin's position, then, it may be helpful to indicate how the philosophical vocabulary of his early fragments is transposed into the "poetological" terminology that characterizes his later essays from the Homburg era. Hölderlin's essay on the "Ground for Empedocles" may serve as a synechdochic instance for this transformation. Speaking of the "General Ground" for his tragedy, Hölderlin remarks that the "image of inwardness," which is tragedy itself, "always denies and must deny its ultimate foundation." The "tragic-dramatic poem" unfolds as the dialectic of the "organic" and the "aorgic," of the reflected and the unreflected principle within the character of the tragic hero. Empedocles, Hölderlin states, "seems indeed born to be a poet." And by way of the "continuous determination of consciousness (. . .) the poet is able to view a totality." However, this totality, which Hölderlin also refers to as "the pure," cannot be "easily conceived of in an idealistic manner." On the contrary, the epoch "demanded a sacrifice." The poet-protagonist Empedocles who progressively determines his "sphere" by absorbing the "destiny of his epoch" realizes the totality of the Fichtean "absolute I" as an individual. Empedocles' destiny thus consists of his determining his "sphere," that is, of his reconciling the "harmonious opposition" between the "aorgic" and the "organic." According to Hölderlin, such an enormous task leads necessarily into the tragic catastrophe.

"Precisely because he expresses the deepest inwardness, the tragic poet"—and here Hölderlin aligns himself explicitly with Empedocles, (and perhaps even with his catastrophic fate)— "denies altogether his individuality or subjectivity." The poet achieves such a presentation of totality by conveying his subjectivity "into a foreign subject matter [*Stoff*]." As the veritable *alter ego* of the poet, such a subject matter clearly exceeds the quality of an aesthetic "option." "The Ground for Empedocles" thus recasts the concept of a "whole" as that of a "sphere;" the absolute determination of this sphere does not coincide with a Fichtean absolute 'I' (a "fact for the philosopher"), but it results in Empedocles' self-destruction. Hölderlin's notion of subject-matter (*Stoff*) as the realm for progressive determination does not imply a Spinozism, a monism or poetic mysticism. For by way of his complex doctrine of the "alternation of tones" Hölderlin reinscribes within the subject-matter itself the dialectic and differentiation which is constitutive of any proper determination. It becomes more and more "reflected and organic."[61] Furthermore, Hölderlin is keenly aware of the fact that not just any subject-matter will be adequate to its task. It is only after an immensely complex examination, whose individual steps are comprised in the dithyrambic opening sentence of Hölderlin's essay on the "Operations of the Poetic Spirit," that the subject-matter can be judged as "receptive."

On a more properly linguistic level, the shift in emphasis from a notion of intuition as *Anschauung* to intuition as an analeptic *Ahndung,* which Hölderlin ascribes to poetic language in his essay "On the Operations of the Poetic Spirit," also indicates the absence of any totalizing figure. It will be the task of a thorough interpretation of Hölderlin's "poetological" writings to show how, on the level of concrete poetic "subject-matter" and "form," Hölderlin's "poetology" outlines a dialectics which no longer aims for its own totalization by way of a restricted linguistic economy. Within the limitations of this introduction, however, we could merely delineate some instances of Hölderlin's doctrine of the alternation of tones and its perpetual "denial of its own foundations" which appears to continue, on the level of the productive *poein,* his earlier scepticism regarding the possibility of a philosophical ontology.

It is the principal purpose of this translation of Hölderlin's theoretical writings, whose significance can no longer be limited to the context of German Idealism, to make accessible to an English readership a unique and intellectually sensitive theoretical oeuvre.[62] While Hölderlin's theoretical and poetological writings have generated a fair amount of critical interest in Germany, the interpretation of the Swabian thinker and poet at the same time has been marred repeatedly by unnecessarily "ideological" positions. Examples would be the question of Hölderlin's so-called "patriotic reversal" (*vaterländische Umkehr*) as well as the incessant philological debate concerning the proper editorial principles for his work. The general tenor of English and American criticism gives reason to hope that such and similar issues may indeed greatly benefit from the ideologically less biased critical perspective of an English audience.

In his famous letter to Böhlendorff, Hölderlin points to an unusual aspect of the continuing "querelle des anciens et modernes" when arguing that "what is familiar must be learned as well as what is foreign." He continues by stating that, indeed, "the use of what is one's own is the most difficult." In keeping with such a position, a truly insightful interpretation of Hölderlin may thus depend on a similar exteriorization, such as accompanies not only translation itself but also any foreign critical reception. "With the exception of what must be the highest for the Greeks and for us—namely, the living relationship and destiny—we must not share anything identical with them." It may prove another Romantic paradox (Hölderlin disclaims: "It sounds paradox") that the interpretation of Hölderlin can only "come into its own" (*das Eigene*) if committed into the hands of the "foreign" (*das Fremde*). However, such a schema which, like Hegel has its interpretive correlate move westward, no longer follows the Hegelian dialectic of history, for here the movement becomes meaningful precisely and only to the extent that it helps us avoid any totalization of the interpreting figure.

ESSAYS

On the Law of Freedom[1]

There is a natural state of the imagination which has in common the lawlessness with that anarchy of representations organized by the intellect, to be sure, yet which, with respect to the law by which it is to be organized, needs to be distinguished from intellect.

By this natural state of imagination, by this lawlessness, I mean a moral one; by this law, [I mean] the law of freedom. There, the imagination is considered in and of itself, here in conjunction with the faculty of desire.

In that anarchy of representations where the imagination is considered theoretically, a unity of the manifold, an ordering of perceptions was indeed possible yet accidental.

In this natural state of fantasy where it [the imagination] is considered in relation to the faculty of desire, moral lawfulness is indeed possible yet accidental.

There is an aspect of the empirical faculty of desire, the analogue of what is called nature, which is most prominent where necessity and freedom, the restricted and the unrestricted, the sensuous and the sacred seem to unite; a natural innocence or, one might say, a morality of the instinct; and the fantasy in tune with it is heavenly.

However this natural state as such is also dependent on natural causes.

It is [a] mere fortune to be thus attuned.

If the law of freedom did not exist where the faculty of desire stood together with fantasy, there would never be a fixed state resembling the one that has just been hinted at; at least,
it would not be up to us to | hold it fast. Likewise, its opposite would occur without us being able to prevent it.

The law of freedom, however, rules without any regard for the help of nature. Nature may or may not be conducive to its

33

enactment, it [the law of freedom] rules. Indeed, it presupposes a resistance in nature, for otherwise it would not rule. The first time that the law of freedom discloses itself to us, it appears as punishing. The origin of all our virtue occurs in evil. Thus morality can never be entrusted to nature. For if morality did not cease to be morality, once its destiny's foundations were located in nature and not in freedom, the legality that could be engendered by mere nature would be a very uncertain thing, changeable according to time and circumstance. As soon as the natural causes would be defined differently, this legality would [. . .]

On the Concept of Punishment[1]

It seems as though the Nemesis of the ancients had been depicted as a daughter of the night less because of her frightfulness than because of her mysterious origin.

It is the necessary fate of all enemies of principles that they end up in a circle with all their claims. (Proof).[2]

In the present case they would sound like this: "Punishment is the suffering of legitimate resistance and the consequence of evil acts. Evil acts, then, are those followed by punishment. And punishment follows where there are evil acts." They could never offer a self-sufficient criterion for an evil act. For if they are consistent, the consequence has to determine the value of the act. To avoid this, they have to proceed from principle. If they do not, and if they determine the value of the act according to its results, then these results—considered in a moral sense—are not founded in anything superior, and the legitimacy of the resistance is nothing more than a word. Punishment is just punishment, and if a mechanism, chance or arbitrariness do something unpleasant to me, I know that I have acted in an evil manner. I have to ask nothing else; what happens, happens rightly so because it happens.

Now, it seems indeed as if something like that was the case where the original concept of punishment occurs, in moral consciousness. There, namely, the moral law announces itself negatively and, as something infinite, cannot announce itself differently. However, as a fact the law is active will. For a law is not active, it is merely the imagined activity. This active will must be directed against another activity of the will. We shall not will something; such is its immediate voice in us. Therefore we have to will something that is opposed to the law of morality.

What the law of morality | is we knew neither before it opposed our will, nor do we know it now that it opposes us; we only experience its resistance as a result of the fact that we willed something which is opposed to the law of morality. According to this result, we determine the value of our will; because we experienced resistance, we consider our will evil; as it seems, we cannot investigate the legitimacy of this resistance any further; and if this is the case, we recognize it [the resistance] only in that we suffer; it does not differ from any other suffering. And for exactly that reason for which I deduce an evil will from the resistance which I call the resistance of the law of morality, I also deduce an evil will from any other resistance. All suffering is punishment.

There is, however, a difference between the cause of cognition and the real cause.* It is nothing less than identical if I say on the one hand: I recognize the law in its resistance and, on the other hand: I acknowledge the law because of its resistance. Those are obliged to perform the above circle for whom the resistance of the law is the real cause. For them the law does not even occur if they do not experience its resistance. Their will is unlawful only because they feel this unlawfulness; if they do not suffer punishment, they are not evil either. Punishment is what follows evil. And evil is what is followed by punishment.

Still, the distinction between a cause of cognition and a real cause seems to be of little help. If the resistance of the law against my will is punishment, and if I recognize the law only with the punishment, the question arises: can I recognize the law through the punishment? and then: can I be punished for transgressing a law of which I was not aware?

To this it may be answered that, insofar as one considers oneself punished, one necessarily implies the transgression of the law within oneself; that in punishment, insofar as one considers it punishment, necessarily [. . .]

---

*ideal [:] without punishment no law
real [:] without law no punishment.[3]

Judgment and Being[1]

Judgment. in the highest and strictest sense, is the original separation of object and subject which are most deeply united in intellectual intuition, that separation through which alone object and subject become possible, the arche-separation. In the concept of separation, there lies already the concept of the reciprocity of object and subject and the necessary presupposition of a whole of which object and subject form the parts. "I am I" is the most fitting example for this concept of arche-separation as *theoretical* separation, for in the practical arche-separation it [the "I"] opposes the *non-I, not itself.*

Reality and potentiality are distinguished like mediate and immediate consciousness. If I think an object as potentiality, I only repeat the preceding consciousness by virtue of which it really is. There is no potentiality conceivable for us that was not reality. Hence the concept of potentiality does not apply to objects of reason, for they never occur in consciousness as what they are supposed to be, but only the concept of necessity [". . . applies to such objects of reason."].[2] The concept of potentiality applies to objects of the intellect, that of reality [applies] to perception and intuition [. . .]

Being—expresses the connection between subject and object. Where subject and object are united altogether and not only in part, that is, united in such a manner that no separation can be performed without violating the essence of what is to be separated, there and nowhere else can be spoken of *Being proper*, as is the case with intellectual intuition.

Yet this Being must not be confused with identity. If I say: I am I, the subject ("I") and the object | ("I") are not united in such a way that no separation could be performed without violating the essence of what is to be separated; on the contrary,

37

the I is only possible by means of this separation of the I from the I. How can I say: "I"! without self-consciousness? Yet how is self-consciousness possible? In opposing myself to myself, separating myself from myself, yet in recognizing myself as the same in the opposed regardless of this separation. Yet to what extent as the same? I can, I must ask in this manner; for in another respect it [the "I"] is opposed to itself. Hence identity is not a union of object and subject which simply occurred, hence identity is not = to absolute Being.

The Perspective from which We Have to Look at Antiquity[1]

We dream of education, piety, p.p. and have none whatsoever; it is appropriated—we dream of originality and autonomy; we believe to be saying all kinds of new things and, still, all this is reaction, as it were, a mild revenge against the slavery with which we have behaved toward antiquity. There seems to be indeed hardly any other choice than to be oppressed by what has been appropriated and by what is positive, or, with violent effort, to oppose as a living force everything learnt, given, positive. What seems most problematic here is that antiquity appears altogether opposed to our primordeal drive which is is bent on forming the unformed, to perfect the primordial-natural so that man, who is born for art, will naturally take to what is raw, uneducated, childlike rather than to a formed material where there has already been pre-formed [what] one wishes to form. And that which was the general reason for the decline of all peoples, namely, that their originality, their own living nature succumbed to the positive forms, to the luxury which their fathers had produced* that seems to be our fate as well, only on a larger scale in that an almost boundless prior world, which we internalize either through learning or through experience, works and exerts pressure on us.** On the other hand, nothing seems to be more favorable than precisely these circumstances in which we find ourselves.[2] ⟨For it makes a difference whether this drive to cultivate operates blindly or with consciousness, whether it knows from where it emerged and whereto it strives; for this is man's only mistake,

---

*examples presented vividly
**demonstration

39

IV,222   that his formative drive goes astray, takes an | unworthy, alto-
gether mistaken direction or, at least, misses its proper place or,
if it has found it, comes to a halt in the middle of the way with
the means that are supposed to lead him to his goal.* That this
happens considerably less frequently** is assured by our knowing
from where and with what goal this formative drive emerges,
that we know the most essential directions along which it moves
toward its goal, that the detours and wrong ways which it can
take are not unknown to us either, that we consider everything
that emerged from that drive before and around us⟩ as having
sprung from the communal, primordial ground from which it
emerges everywhere with all its products; that we recognize around
us the most essential directions which it took before and with
us, also its aberrations, and now, for the same reason which we
assume as the vivid and universally equal origin of all formative
drives, give ourselves our own direction which is determined by
the preceding pure and impure directions that we, due to understanding, do not repeat*** so that in the *primordial foundation
of all works and acts of man we feel ourselves to be equal and at
one with all, be they so large or small,* yet in the particular direction
which we take**** [. . .]

---

*examples vivid.
**to be examined especially.
***the pure directions we do not repeat, because [. . .]
****our particular direction *To Act.* Reaction against positive animation of
what is dead through *authentic mutual union* ("reelle Wechselvereinigung") of
the two.

❧

On the Different Forms of Poetic Composition[1]

Occasionally one is in disagreement with oneself about the good qualities of various people. Each one has his excellence and with it his personal shortcomings. This person pleases us through the simplicity, accuracy, and ease with which he moves in a specific direction to which he devoted himself. The moments of his life follow one another without interruption and with ease; everything has its place and time for him; nothing waivers, nothing interferes, and because he remains with the ordinary he is hardly ever exposed to great effort and great doubt. Determined, clear, always the same and moderate, and adequate to the place and the moment and entirely within the present, he is never—if we are not too tense or high strung—an inconvenience for us; he leaves us as we are, we get along with him easily; he does not advance us by much, in fact, does not really interest us very deeply; but we do not always wish that either, and especially when overcome by violent disturbances we have at first no more genuine need than just such company, such an object with which we will recover ourselves in an equilibrium, in calmness and clarity.

We call the described character preferably *natural*, and we are right with this homage at least to the same extent as one of the seven sages who, in his language and mode of conceptualization, claimed that everything—had originated out of water. For if, within the moral world, nature in its progress always proceeds from the simplest situations and forms of life, as seems to be the case, then those plain characters have to be called not without reason the most primordial, the most natural ones.

| [. . .[2]] has agreed, then it is necessary for everyone who wants to state his opinion about this matter to explain himself at first in firm concepts and words.

Thus here as well.

The natural tone, which is particularly proper to the epic, is already recognizable in its outward appearance.

One passage of Homer allows one to say what can be said of this tone in general. (As indeed in a good poem, one period of speech can represent the entire work, thus we also find it in this tone and this poem.). For this purpose, I select the speech of Phoenix where he wants to move the furious Achilleus to be reconciled with Agamemmnon and to help in the fight against the Trojans.

[*Iliad*, IX, 485–498]*

IV,230 |The explicit, continuous, and genuinely true tone becomes readily apparent.

And thus the epic poem, too, adheres to reality in the larger sense. It is, if one (merely) considers its peculiarity, a character-painting; and indeed, when looked at from this point of view, the Iliad explains itself from all sides.** In a character-painting, then, all other qualities of the natural tone are at their essential place. This *visible* sensuous unity, where everything predominantly emerges from and returns to the hero, where beginning and catastrophe and end are tied to him, where all the characters and situations in all their multiplicity and with everything that happens or is said are directed, like the points of a line, toward the moment when he appears in his highest individuality, *this* unity, as can easily be understood, is possible only in a work which sees its true purpose in the presentation of characters, and where hence the main source rests in the main character.

Thus from this point, there follows the calmer moderation which is so proper to the natural tone, which shows the characters within their boundaries and gently subdivides them into various shades. The artist is not this moderate in the poetic form because he considers this procedure the only poetic one; for instance, he

---

*I need to tell only few people that this is the Voss translation, and to those who do not yet know it, I admit that I, too, to my great regret, have only recently become familiar with it.[3]

**And if the incidents and circumstances wherein the characters present themselves are developed so extensively, this is so primarily because the former—without being altered or propelled out of the ordinary mood or form—appear in this manner precisely to the human beings which live within them.

avoids the extremes and oppositions not because he does not want to use them under any circumstance; he knows well that in the right place there exist poetically true extremes and oppositions of characters, events, thoughts, passions, images, of sensations; he only excludes them to the extent that they do not fit in with the present work; he had to choose a fixed point of view, and that is now the individual, the character of his hero, as he has gained a determinate personal existence, a reality by means of nature and education. However, precisely this individuality of the character is necessarily lost | in extremes. If Homer had not removed Achilleus so gently-carefully from the turmoil, we would hardly distinguish the gods' son from the elements surrounding him; and only where we find him calm in his camp delighting his heart with the lyre and singing the victorious deeds of the men with Patroclos sitting across from him, waiting in silence until he has finished his song, only here do we have the youth presented properly.

V,231

Thus, it is in order to preserve the individuality of the presented character, which is what right now he is most concerned with, that the epic poet is so very moderate.

And if the circumstances in which the epic characters exist are presented so accurately and extensively, it is once again not because the poet places all poetic value in this circumstantiality. In a different situation, he would avoid it to a certain degree; yet here, where his perspective is individuality, authenticity, determinate existence of the characters, the surrounding world, too, has to appear in this perspective. And if the surrounding objects are presented so accurately and extensively, it is once again not because the poet places all poetic value in this circumstantiality. In a different situation, he would avoid it to a certain degree; yet here, where his perspective is individuality, authenticity, determinate existence of the characters, the surrounding world, too, has to appear in this perspective. And that, from this perspective, the surrounding objects appear precisely in such exactness, we experience for ourselves whenever, in our own most ordinary mood and without being disturbed, we are present to the circumstances under which we exist.

I would like to add a good deal more, if I was not afraid of digressing. Still, I add that this explicitness in the presented circumstances is a mere reflex of the characters insofar as they

are generally individuals and not yet more specifically determined. The surrounding can be fitted the character in yet another
way. In the Iliad, the individuality of Achilles, which surely is
made for this purpose, imparts itself to everything and anybody,
to what surrounds him and not just to the circumstances but to
the characters as well. At the contests that are being held in
honor of the dead Patroklos, almost all other heroes of the Greek
army wear more or less noticeably his color, and finally the old
Priam in all his suffering appears to rejuvenate in front of the
youth who, after all, was his enemy.

IV,232 | Yet one will readily notice that this latter [observation]
already moves beyond the natural tone as it has been viewed and
described so far, in its *mere* singularity.

In this respect, then, it already affects us positively by virtue
of its explicitness, its continuous changes, its reality.

Reflection[1]

There are degrees of enthusiasm. From the gaiety, which is probably the lowest, up the the enthusiasm of the general who in the midst of the battle maintains his genius with presence of mind, there exists an infinite ladder. To mount up and down on this ladder is the vocation and delight of the poet.

. . .

One has inversions of words in the period.[2] Yet the inversion of the periods itself, then, must prove greater and more effective. The logical position of periods where the ground (the grounding period) is followed by becoming, becoming by the goal, the goal by the purpose, and where the subclauses are always only attached at the end of the main clauses to which they refer—is certainly only very seldom of use to the poet.

. . .

That is the measure of enthusiasm which is given to every individual, that the one keeps the presence of mind to the necessary degree in greater, the other one only in smaller fire. Where temperance forsakes you, there are the boundaries of your enthusiasm. The great poet is never abandoned by himself; he may elevate himself as far above himself as he wishes. One can fall upward just as well as downward. The latter is prevented by the flexible spirit, the former by the gravity that lies in temperate presence of mind. However, feeling is probably the best temperance and presence of mind for the poet, if it is authentic, warm, clear and strong. It is the spirit's bridle and spur. It impells the spirit with warmth, [and] it defines its boundary with tenderness, authenticity, clearity and restrains it so that it does not go

45

astray; and thus it is at once understanding and will. However, if it is too tender and effeminate, then it becomes deadly, a nagging worm. If the spirit restricts itself, then it [feeling] senses too anxiously the | momentary restriction, becomes too warm, looses the clearity, and impels the spirit with an incomprehensible restlessness into the unlimited; if the spirit is more free, and if it lifts itself instantly above the rule and the subject matter, then it [feeling] becomes likewise anxious, fears going astray as it feared the restrictedness before; it [feeling] becomes cold and dull, wears on the spirit so that it sinks, hesitates and labors under superfluous doubt. Once feeling is that ill, the poet, because he knows it, can do nothing better than to never let himself be frightened by it and to respect it only insofar as he proceeds somewhat more restrained and uses his understanding as readily as possible in order to immediately correct the impression that it [feeling] be restricting or liberating, and—once he has repeatedly helped himself out in this manner—to restore to feeling the natural certainty and consistency. Overall, he must accustom himself not to try to attain within individual moments the totality that he strives for and to bear the momentarily incomplete; it must be his delight that he surpass himself from one moment to the next to the degree and in the manner required by the subject matter, until in the end the principal tone of his totality succeeds. However, he must by no means think that he can only supercede himself in the *crescendo* from the weaker to the stronger; in that manner he will become inauthentic and too high-strung; he must feel that he is gaining in levity what he has lost in significance, that silence and the sensuous replace the vehemence and the impetus quite beautifully, and thus the progression of the work will not involve one necessary tone which, as it were, did not already surpass the preceding one; and the dominant tone will be such only because the whole is composed in this and no other manner.

IV,234

. . .

Only that is the most veritable truth wherein even error—because it is posited in the whole of its system, in its time and space—becomes truth. It [truth] is the light that illuminates itself and the night as well. This, too, is the highest poesy in which even the unpoetic—because it is said at the right time and at the right place within the whole of the | work of art—becomes poetic. Yet for this purpose quick understanding is most necessary. How can you need the matter at the right place, if you still linger shyly over it and do not know how much there is to it, how much or how little can be made of it. That is eternal gaiety, that is joy of God, that one places everything individual in its proper place within the whole; hence, without understanding or without a feeling that is organized through and through [there is] no excellence, no life.

. . .

Must man really loose in flexibility of strength and sense what he gains in all-encompassing spirit? After all, neither is anything without the other!

. . .

It is with joy that you must understand the pure as such, man, and other beings, must receive "everything essential and characteristic" of the former, and must recognize all relations, one after another, and repeat their constituents in their coherence so long for yourself until the living intuition again emerges *more objectively* from thought, from joy, before necessity sets in; the understanding which emerges merely out of necessity is always distorted towards one side.

Whereas love likes to discover with tenderness (unless the soul and the senses have become shy and dull through severe fates and monk's morals) and will not overlook anything, and where it discovers so-called errors or mistakes (parts which in what they are or through their position and movement momentarily diverge from the tone of the whole), feels and intuits the whole only more intrinsically.[3] Hence all cognition should begin with the study of the beautiful. For he has gained much who can understand life without grieving. Furthermore, enthusiasm and passion are also good, devotion which life will not touch, recognize, and then desperation when life itself emerges from its

IV,235

infinity. The deep sense of mortality, of change, of his temporal limitations enflames man so that he attempts much; [it] exercises all his powers, and prevents him from idleness, and one struggles for chimeras so long until again | something true and authentic is found for cognition and occupation. In good times there are seldom any enthusiasts. Yet when man lacks great, pure objects then he creates some phantom out of this or that and closes the eyes in order to be able to take interest in it and live for it.

IV,236

. . .

Everything depends on that those who excel and the more beautiful ones do not exclude too much from themselves that which is inferior and barbaric, nor mingle too much with it, *that they recognize with determination and without passion the distance which exists between them and the other ones, and that they work and tolerate out of this knowledge.* If they isolate themselves too much, then the effectiveness is lost and they perish in their solitude. If they mingle too much, then again no real effectiveness is possible, for either they speak and act against the other ones as against their own kind and overlook the point where the latter are deficient and where they need to be seized first, or they adjust too much to the latter and repeat the impropriety which they are supposed to purge; in either case they effect nothing and must perish, because they either express themselves forever into the blue and remain in solitude with all struggle and begging, or because they adapt with too much servility what is strange and more common, and thus are suffocated by it.

The Sages, however, . . .[1]

The sages, however, who differentiate only with the spirit, [and] only universally hasten quickly back into pure Being and fall into an all the greater indifference because they believe to have differentiated, and because they take the non-opposition to which they have returned for an eternal one. They have deceived their nature with the lowest degree of reality, with the shadow of reality, the ideal opposition and differentiation, and nature takes revenge by [. . .]

②

The Ground for "Empedocles"[1]

The tragic ode begins in the highest fire; the pure spirit, the pure inwardness has transcended its border, it has not sufficiently moderated those connections of life which are necessary and which, as it is, already strive for contact, and which are excessively inclined to do so due to the wholly inward mood, [that is] consciousness, reflection, or physical sensuousness; and thus, through the excess of inwardness, there has originated a discord which the tragic ode figures forth right at the outset in order to depict the pure. The ode then moves by way of a natural act from the extreme of differentiation and of necessity to the extreme of non-differentiation of the pure, of the supernatural which does not seem to acknowledge any necessity whatsoever; from there it falls into a pure sensuousness, into a more moderate inwardness, for the originally higher, more divine and daring inwardness has appeared to the ode as an extreme; nor can the ode any longer fall into that degree of excessive inwardness with which it set out in its initial tone, for it has experienced, one might say, whereto this would lead, and it must transcend the extremes of differentiation and non-differentiation into that quiet thoughtfulness and sensitivity where it necessarily must feel the struggle of the more forced thoughtfulness, hence has to accept its initial tone and proper character as opposites and has to transcend toward the latter if it is not to end tragically in this restrictedness; however, because it senses the initial tone to be opposed, the idealistic, which unites the two opposites, emerges more purely, the original tone is recovered, namely with thoughtfulness, and thus it proceeds from there through a moderate, freer reflection or sensation, in a more secure, free, and profound manner (that is, out of the experience and recognition of heterogeneity) back to the initial tone.

V,150 | **General Ground**

It is the most profound inwardness which is expressed in the tragic dramatic poem. The tragic ode presents inwardness also in the most positive distinctions, in true oppositions; however, these oppositions exist still more as form and as the immediate language of sensation. The tragic poem veils inwardness in the presentation even more, expresses it through stronger distinctions, because it expresses a more profound inwardness, a more infinite divinity. The sensation is no longer expressed in an immediate manner; it is no longer the poet and his own experience which appear—even though every poem, thus also the tragic one must have emerged from poetic life and reality, from the poet's own world and soul—because otherwise the veritable truth will be missing; and nothing whatsoever can be understood and animated, if we cannot translate our own mood and experience into an foreign analogical subject matter. Thus, the divine which the poet senses and experiences in his world is also expressed in the tragic-dramatic poem; for him the tragic-dramatic poem, too, is an image of life which is and was present to him in his life; yet to the extent that this image of inwardness always denies and must deny its ultimate foundation, to the extent that everywhere it approaches increasingly the symbol, the more infinite, unspeakable, the closer that inwardness is to the *nefas*, the stricter and colder the image separates man and his felt element in order to contain the sensation within its boundaries, the less the image can express the sensation in an immediate manner; it must deny it with regard to form as well as to subject matter; the subject matter must be a more daring and foreign parable and example of it; the form must bear more the character of the opposition and separation. Another world, other events, foreign characters, yet like every more daring parable, all the more closely adapted to the basic subject matter, and heterogeneous only in the outer appearance; for if this intrinsic kinship of the parable with the subject matter, the characteristic inwardness which | is the foundation of the image were not visible, then its remoteness, its foreign form could not be explained. The more foreign they are, the more lively the foreign forms have to be, and the less the

V,151

visible subject matter of the poem resembles the subject matter that underlies the mood and the world of the poet, the less may the spirit, the divine—as felt by the poet in his world—be denied in the artistic, foreign subject matter. However, also in this foreign, artistic subject matter, inwardness, the divine may not and cannot be expressed other than through a differentiation all the greater, the more intimate the founding sensation is. Hence 1) tragedy is dramatic with regard to its subject matter and form, i.e., a) it contains a third, more foreign subject matter, different from the poet's own mood and world, which he selected because he considered it sufficiently analogical as to convey into it and preserve in there, like in a vessel, his total sensation, and [this] all the safer, the less familiar the subject matter is to this analogy; for the most intimate sensation is exposed to transitoriness precisely to that degree to which it does not deny the true temporal and sensuous relations (and it is therefore lyric law—since inwardness as such can be maintained there less profoundly and hence more easily—to deny the physical and intellectual interrelation). Precisely because he expresses the deepest inwardness, the tragic poet denies altogether his individuality, his subjectivity, and thus also the object present to him; he conveys them into a foreign personality, into a foreign objectivity (and even where the fundamental total sensation is betrayed most clearly, in the principal character which sets the tone of the drama, and in the central scene where the object of the drama, destiny expresses its secret most clearly, where it assumes most strongly the appearance of homogeneity against its hero (which is precisely what seizes him most strongly), even there[2]

IV,152 | [. . .] and fatal success which attaches to false attempts for a restored pure inwardness in the soul, not again dealt with autonomously by the suffering through a new appropriate, inappropriate attempt, but is performed proleptically by another one which moves precisely along that way, only standing a step higher or lower so that the soul affected by false attempts of improvement is not only disturbed by its own activity but even more altered and inclined to a vehement reaction by the sudden intrusion of another activity.

Ground for Empedocles

In pure life, nature and art are only opposed harmoniously. Art is the blossom, the perfection of nature; nature only becomes divine in conjunction with the diverse yet harmonious art; when everything is entirely what it can be, and one combines with the other, compensates for the shortcomings of the other, which that one must necessarily have in order to be entirely that which it can be as a particular, then there exists perfection, and the divine rests in between the two. The more organic, artistic man is the blossom of nature, the more aorgic[3] nature, when it is sensed purely, by the purely organized, purely and uniquely formed man, affords him the feeling of perfection. However, this life exists only in sentiment and not for knowledge. If it is to be known, then it must present itself by separating itself in the excess of inwardness where the opposed principles interchange so that the organic, which surrendered itself too much to nature,

√,153 | and which forgot its essence and consciousness, transcends into the extreme of autonomous activity and art and reflection, whereas nature, at least in its effects on reflective man, transcends into the extreme of the aorgic, the incomprehensible, the non-sensuous, the unlimited, until through the progression of the opposed reciprocal effects the two originally united [principles] meet again as in the beginning, only that nature has become more organic through the forming, cultivating man, through the formgiving drives and forces as such,[4] whereas man has become more aorgic, universal, infinite. This sentiment probably belongs to the highest that can be felt, when both opposed [principles], the universalized, spiritually vital, artificially, purely aorgic man and the beautiful appearance of nature encounter each other. This sentiment probably belongs to the highest that man can experience, for the present harmony reminds him of the previous, reversed, pure relation, and he feels himself and nature in a double sense, and the connection is more infinite.

In the middle there lies the struggle and the death of the individual, that moment when the organic discards its subjectivity, its particular existence which had become an extreme, when the aorgic discards its universality not, as in the beginning, by way of an idealistic fusion but in real, supreme struggle, in that the particular at its extreme must increasingly and actively universalize itself against the extreme of the aorgic, must increasingly rend away from its center, whereas the aorgic must increasingly concentrate against the extreme of the particular and must gain a center and become the most particular; where, then, the organic that has turned aorgic appears to find and return to itself in that it keeps to the individuality of the aorgic, and where the object, the aorgic appears to find itself in that at the very same moment that it assumes individuality it also finds the organic at the highest extreme of the aorgic, so that at this moment, *at this birth of the highest hostility | the highest reconciliation appears to be the case.* Yet the individuality of this moment is only a product of the highest struggle, its universality only a product of the highest struggle; in the way that reconciliation seems to be there and that the organic and the aorgic in their respective manner work toward this moment, the individuality of aorgic origin which is contained within the moment becomes—based on the impressions of the organic—again more aorgic; based on the impressions of the organic, the universality of organic origin becomes more particular, so that the uniting moment dissolves more and more, like a phantasm, reacts against the organic in aorgic manner, distances itself from it; however due to this and to its death it [the moment] reconciles and unites the contending extremes out of which it emerged more beautifully than during its lifetime, in that now the union occurs not in a particular and thus is too close, in that the divine no longer appears in sensuous manner, in that the happy deceit of the union ceases precisely to the extent that it was too close and unique, so that both extremes of which one, the organic, must be deterred by the transitory moment and thus be raised to a purer universality, while the aorgic one, transcending to the former, must become an object of calmer contemplation for the organic, and that the inwardness of the past moment emerges in more universal, controlled, differentiating, clearer manner.

IV,154

Thus Empedocles is a son of his heaven and his time, of his fatherland, a son of tremendous oppositions of nature and art in which the world appeared before his eyes.[5] A man within whom those oppositions are united *so* intimately that they become

one within him, that they discard and reverse their originally differentiating form, that what is considered more subjective in his world and exists more in particularity, [namely], differentiation, thinking, comparing, forming, organizing and being organized, are more objective within himself so that he, in order to name it as strongly as possible, is more differentiating, thinking, comparing, | forming, organizing and organized, when he is less with himself; and, insofar as he is less conscious of the fact that with and for him the speechless gains speech, that with and for him the universal, the less conscious gains the form of consciousness and particularity, that, in contrast, that which for others in his world counts as more objective and exists in more universal form, the less differentiating and differentiable, the less reflected, less comparable, the less figurative, the unorganized and the disorganizing is with and for him more subjective; that he is less undifferentiated and undifferentiating, less calculated in effect, more incomparable, unformed, aorgic and dis-organic, if he is more with himself, and—if and insofar as he is more conscious—that with and for him the speaking becomes unspeakable or not-to-be spoken, that with him and for him the particular and more conscious takes on the form of the unconscious, hence that those two contraries become one within him and also unite insofar as they are different in the original sentiment—
such a human being can only grow out of the highest opposition of nature and art, and as, (ideally), the excess of inwardness emerges out of inwardness, so *this real excess of inwardness* emerges from hostility and highest antagonism where the aorgic takes on the moderate appearance of the particular and seems to reconcile with the super-organic, where the organic in turn takes on the moderate appearance of the universal and appears to be reconciled with the super-aorgic, super-animated, only because both interpenetrate and meet each other most intensely at their highest extreme and thus have to take on in their outer form the appearance, the semblance of opposition.

Thus Empedocles is, as we said, the result of his time, and his character points back to it just as it emerged from it. His fate presents itself to him in a momentary union which, however, has to dissolve, though, in order to increase.

| He seems indeed born to be a poet, thus seems to possess

in his subjective, more active nature that uncommon tendency toward universality which, under other circumstances or through circumspection and avoidance of its too powerful influence, becomes that completeness and continuous determination of consciousness by means of which the poet is able to view a *totality*; likewise, there seems to lie in his objective nature, in his passivity that fortunate gift which, even without conscientious and competent ordering, thinking, and forming, is inclined to order, think, and form, that formative capacity[6] of the senses and the soul which quickly and without effort takes in all such matter in its totality, and which endows artistic activity more the power to speak than to act. However, this talent should not work and remain in its peculiar sphere; he [Empodecles] should not work in his manner and measure, in his distinctive restrictedness and purity and, by expressing this mood freely, allow it to become a more universal one which at the same time was the destiny of his people; the destiny of his epoch, the tremendous extremes out of which he grew, did not demand a song where the pure is still easily conceived in an idealistic presentation which rests between the appearance of destiny and the original, if time has not yet too much moved away from it; neither did the destiny of his epoch demand the true action which takes effect and helps immediately, to be sure, though also more one-sidedly and all the more the less it exposes man; it demanded a sacrifice where man in his entirety becomes real and visible as that wherein the destiny of his epoch seems to dissolve, where the extremes seem to unite truly and visibly in one but therefore are united too closely; and where in an idealistic action the individual perishes and must perish because the latter showed the premature, sensuous union effected by necessity and antagonism which dissolved the problem of destiny which, however, can never dissolve visibly and individually, because otherwise the universal would be lost

in the individual and (which is even | worse than all great movements of destiny and by itself impossible) the life of a world would expire in some particular instance; whereas, if this instance dissolves as the premature result of destiny, because it was too inward, real and visible, the problem of destiny is solved in the same manner as regards material yet in a different manner as regards form; for the excess of inwardness which emerged by chance—yet originally did so only as an ideal and as an attempt— and which has now become real by way of the highest antago- nism, cancels itself, precisely for that reason, the degrees, forces, and mechanisms in which the original excess of inwardness, the cause of all antagonism was cancelled, so that the force of inward excess dissipates and a more mature, truthful, pure, universal inwardness remains.

Thus Empedocles was supposed to become a victim of his time. The problems of the destiny in which he matured were to resolve seemingly within him, and this solution was to present itself as a seemingly temporary one—as is the case with more or less all tragic individuals who in their characters and utterances are all more or less attempts to solve the problems of destiny, and who are cancelled to the extent that they are not universally valid unless, on the other hand, their role, their character and its utterances present themselves as something transient and momentary, so that the one who seemingly solves destiny most completely also presents himself most clearly in his transitoriness and, in the progress of his attempts, most evidently as victim.

How, then, is this the case with Empedocles?

The more powerful destiny, the opposites of art and nature were, the more it was their potential to individualize themselves increasingly, to gain a fixed point, a hold, and such a time seizes all individuals so long, challenges them to a solution until some- thing is found in which their unknown need and their secret tendency manifests itself visibly and as achieved, from which point, then, the found solution must transcend into the universal.

V,158 | Thus his time is individualized in Empedocles, and the more it is individualized in him, the brighter and more real and visible the riddle appears solved within him, the more necessary becomes his ruin.

(1) Already the lively, all-endeavoring spirit of art in his people in general had to be repeated within him in a more aorgic, daring, unrestricted manner, as, on the other hand, the glowing streak of light and the opulent Sicilian nature had to present themselves more felt, speaking for him and within him; and once he was seized by both sides, the one side, the more active force of his being, always had to strengthen as counterforce the other one, just as the spirit of art had to be nourished and driven on

by the feeling part of his soul. —(2) Among his hyper-political, ever judging and calculating Agrigentians, among the progressive and ever renewing social forms of his city, a spirit such as his, which always strove for the creation of a complete whole, had to become all too much a reformer's spirit, just as the anarchic autonomy where everyone followed his originality without paying attention to the peculiarity of the others had to render him with his rich, self-contained nature and plenitude of life, more proud and individual than others; and these two aspects of his character, too, had to elevate and transcend each other reciprocally. (3) A free-spirited boldness which increasingly opposes the unknown, lying outside of human consciousness and activity, the more closely people at first found themselves united with that unknown and driven by a natural instinct to protect themselves against the too mighty, too deep, friendly influence of the element, against self-forgetfulness and total objectivation, this free-spirited boldness, this negative reasoning, non-thinking of the unknown which is so natural among a presumptious people had to move one step further with Empedocles who in no case was made for negation; he had to try to master the unknown, | want to assure himself of it, his spirit had to counteract the servility so much that it would inevitably attempt to enclose the overwhelming nature, to completely understand and become conscious of it as he could be conscious and certain of himself; he had to struggle with it for identity; thus his spirit had to assume aorgic form, to rend away from itself and its center, to penetrate its object so excessively that it would lose itself within it as in an abyss, whereas the entire life of the object, then, could seize the abandoned soul which had become only infinitely more receptive through the infinite activity of the spirit, and where it had to become individuality, had to yield it its particularity and harmonize it more sustainedly since it [his spirit] had given itself in spiritually active manner to the object, and thus the object appeared within the spirit in subjective form just as the spirit had assumed the objective form of the object itself. It [the spirit] was the universal, the unknown, the object was the particular. And thus the conflict involving art, thinking, the ordering of the form-giving human character, and the less conscious nature appeared to be resolved,

IV,159

appeared to be blended into one at the highest extremes and to the point of exchange of the reciprocal, differentiating form. This was the magic with which Empedocles appeared in his world. Nature, which with its might and charms dominated his free-spirited contemporaries only the more, the less discernibly they abstracted from it; nature appeared with all her melodies through the spirit and word of this man and so intimate, warm, and personal as if his heart was hers and the spirit of the element lived among mortals in human form. This gave him his grace, his dreadfulness, his divinity, and all hearts which were moved by the storm of destiny, and spirits which erred back and forth inconstantly and without guidance in the strange night of the time, flew toward him; and the more humanely, the closer to their nature he joined them, the more, with this soul, he made their case his, and after his soul appeared once in his divine form and now | was restored to them in its more proper form, the more he was the venerated one. This basic tone of his character became manifest in all its situations. They all assimilated it. Thus he lived in his highest independence, under a condition which, also without the more objective and historical conditions, prescribed his course such that the external circumstances which led him onto the same course—however essential and indispensable they are for bringing out and into play what, perhaps, would have remained but a thought for him—that the external conditions, despite all opposition in which he subsequently appears to exist with them, meet with his freest mood and soul, which no longer comes as a surprise, since it is precisely this mood which forms the innermost spirit of the circumstances, for all extremes in these circumstances emerged from and returned to precisely this spirit. In his most independent situation the destiny of his epoch resolves in the first and last problem; just as this seeming solution begins from here on to suspend itself and thus to end.

In this independent situation he lives, in that highest inwardness which provides for the basic tone of his character, together with the elements, meanwhile the world around him exists exactly in the highest opposition, in that free-spirited non-thinking, not-accepting of life on the one hand, in the highest servility against the influences of nature, on the other hand. In

IV, 160

this situation he lives (1) generally as feeling man, (2) as philosopher and poet, (3) as a solitary man attending to his gardens.
Yet still he would not be a dramatic person; hence he must solve
destiny not just in universal situations and through his independent character, he must solve it in particular situations and
with the most specific motivation and task. However, as intrinsic
a relation as he bears to the life of the elements, he also bears
to his people. He was not capable of the violent spirit of reno-
vation which moves against the spiteful, anarchic life which will
tolerate no influence, no art, which only strives by way of opposition; he had to move one step further; in order to organize life,
IV,161   he had to | strive seizing it with his being at its innermost; with
his spirit he had to try to master the human element, all tendencies and drives, their soul, the inconceivable, the unconscious,
the involuntary in them; precisely in so far as his will, his consciousness, his spirit, transcended the ordinary and human
boundaries of knowledge and effectiveness, it had to lose itself
and become objective; and what he wanted to give he had to
find, whereas the objective resounded the more purely and deeply
within him the more open his soul lay, precisely because the
spiritually active man had given himself away, and this in the
particular as well as in the universal.

As religious reformer, as political man, and in all actions
which he did for their sake, he therefore behaved toward them
with this proud, enthusiastic devotion, and thus all destiny was
already dissolved through the expression of this reversal between
object and subject. Yet, what can this expression consist of?
Which [expression], in such a relation, suffices for that part which
initially is the incredulous one? and everything lies in this expression, for that unifying [principle] must perish because it appeared
too visibly and sensuously, and this it can only do by expressing
itself at some most determinate point and instance. They have
to see the unity that exists between them and the man; how can
they? in that he obeys them to the extremest degree? yet wherein?
With regard to a matter where they are most doubtful about the
union of the extremes in which they live. Now, if these extremes
consist in the opposition of art and nature, then he must reconcile
nature with art precisely where it is most inaccessible to art,
before its very eyes. —From here the plot evolves. He does it

IV,162

with love and reluctance,* passes his test; now they consider everything | completed. He recognizes them in it. The delusion with which he lived, as though he was at one with them, now ceases. He withdraws and they turn cold against him. His enemy makes use of that, effects the forced exile. His enemy, like Empedocles great in natural talents, seeks to solve the problems of the time in a different, more negative way. Born to be a hero, he is not inclined to unite the extremes and at the same time tame them and tie their reciprocity to something permanent and stable that is posited between them and keeps each of them within its boundaries in that it appropriates each of them. His virtue is understanding, his goddess necessity. He is destiny itself, only with the exception that the contending forces inside him are tied to a consciousness, to a point of separation which keeps them facing one another in clear and controlled manner, which ties them to a (negative) ideality and gives them a direction. In the way that with Empedocles art and nature are reunited at the extreme of their opposition, that the active principle becomes excessively objective and that the lost subjectivity is replaced by the profound effect of the object, so art and nature are united in his enemy—[namely] that an excess of objectivity and being-outside-oneself and reality (in such climate, in such turmoil of passions and change of originality, in such despotic dread of the unknown) has to take the place of the active and forming principle in a daring, open soul, whereas the subjective takes on more the passive appearance of suffering, endurance, firmness, assuredness; and if the extremes assume the appearance of the calm and organic, either because of their gift for endurance of the former or even from the outside, then the subjective-active must now become the organizing [principle], must become the element, thus also confuse the subjective and objective in their appearance and become one with them.

---

*for the fright of becoming positive must naturally be his greatest, out of the sense that *He*, the more authentic he expresses the intimate the more certain he will perish.

On the Operations of the
Poetic Spirit[1]

Once the poet is in control of the spirit, once he has felt and appropriated, has held fast and assured himself of the communal soul which common to everyone and proper to each, once he is furthermore certain of the free movement, of the harmonious alternation and progressive striving wherein the spirit tends to reproduce itself within itself and others, once he is certain of the beautiful progress and its poetic mode of conclusion pre-scribed by the spirit's ideal, once he has realized that a conflict is necessary between the most original postulate of the spirit which aims at [the] communality and unified simultaneity of all parts, and the other postulate which commands the spirit to move beyond itself and reproduce itself, within itself and others, through a beautiful progression and alternation, when this strug-gle continually grasps and pulls him on the way toward enact-ment; once he has further realized that, on the one hand, such communality and interrelation of all parts, such spiritual import would not be tangible if these—even when discounting the har-monious alternation, and also given the permanence of that spiritual form (of coincidence and coexistence)—were not dif-ferent in degree, as regards sensuous import, so that furthermore the harmonious change, that striving was once again intangible and an empty, a facile shadow-play, if the alternating parts—considering also the difference of the sensuous import—do not remain equal to each other in the sensuous form under the alter-nation and striving, once he has realized that the very struggle between spiritual content (between the interrelation of all parts) and spiritual form (the alternation of all parts), between the remaining and striving of the spirit be resolved in that during
the striving of the spirit, | during the alternation of the spiritual

form, the form of the subject matter remain identical in all parts, and that it replace as much as was lost of the original relation and unity of the parts during the harmonious alternation, that it constitute the objective content in contrast to the spiritual form, and that the latter lend it its full significance; that, on the other hand, the material alternation of the subject matter which accompanies the eternal of the spiritual content, that its manifold nature satisfy the demands of the spirit which the latter makes during its progression and which are impeded at every moment by the postulate of unity and eternity, that precisely this material change constitute the objective form, the appearance in contrast to the spiritual content; on the other hand, if he has realized that the struggle between the material alternation and the material identity ought to be resolved in that the loss of material

IV,243   identity,* of passionate progress fleeing discontinuity, | was replaced with the ever-resounding, all-balancing spiritual content, and that the loss of material variety effected by the quicker

---

*material identity? originally, it must be that in the subject matter before the material alternation which, in the spirit, is the unity prior to the idealistic alternation; it must be the sensuous point of contact for all parts. For like the spirit, the subject matter must also be appropriated and held fast by the poet with free interest once it is present in its full nature, once the impression that it [the subject matter] makes on the poet, the first delight, which could be accidental, has been investigated and has been found receptive for the spirit's treatment, and effective, appropriate for the spirit to reproduce itself within itself and others; once, after this investigation, it is again sensed and evoked in all its parts and engaged in an as yet unexpressed, felt effect. And actually this effect is the identity of the subject matter, because within it all parts are concentrated. because within it all parts are concentrated. Yet it is left too unspecified; the subject matter still remains undeveloped. It must be expressed clearly in all its parts and therefore must be weakened in the liveliness of its total impression. The subject matter needs to do this, for in the unexpressed effect it is present to the poet, to be sure, yet not to others; furthermore the spirit has not yet truly reproduced this in the unexpressed effect, it only affords him the capability, which rests in the subject matter, to form knowledge and to realize a striving, reproduction. The subject matter, then, must | be distributed, the overall impression must be suspended, and identity must become a striving from one point to the next where the overall impression is found such that beginning, middle and end bear the most intrinsic relation to one another, so that in the conclusion the end returns to the beginning and the latter to the middle.

striving toward the center and [an] impression, and by this material identity, that this loss is replaced by the ever-changing ideal spiritual form;[2] once he has realized how, conversely, the conflict between spiritual, tranquil content and spiritual, alternating form, insofar as they are irreconcilable, and thus also the conflict between material alternation and material, identical striving toward the principal moment, insofar as they are irreconcilable, renders tangible one as well as the other, once he has finally realized how the conflict of the spiritual content and the idealistic form on the one hand, and between the material alternation and identical striving on the other hand, unite in points of rest and principal moments, and how, to the extent that they cannot be reconciled [the points of rest and principal moments] also become tangible and are felt within these, once he has realized all this, then he is only concerned with the receptivity of the subject matter to the ideal content and the ideal form. If he is assured and in control of both, of the receptivity of the subject matter as well as of the spirit, then neither can be missing in the principal moment.

What, then, must the subject matter be like which is especially receptive to the ideal, to its content, to metaphor and its form, its transition?

The subject matter is either a sequence of events or perspectives, realities, to be described, painted in subjective or objective manner, or it is a sequence of desires, representations, thoughts, or passions, necessities, to be coded in subjective or objective manner, or a sequence of fictions and possibilities, to

IV,244 | be formed subjectively or objectively.* In all three cases it must be capable of the ideal treatment, namely, if there exists an authentic cause for the events, perspectives which are to be narrated, described, or for the thoughts and passions which are to be drawn, or for the fictions which are to be formed, if the events or perspectives emerge from genuine aspirations, the

---

*If the sentiment constitutes significance, the presentation is visual and the spiritual treatment becomes manifest in episodic manner.

If the intellectual intuition constitutes significance, the expression, the material is passionate; the spiritual treatment manifests itself more in style.

If the significance is a more specific purpose, the expression is sensuous, the free treatment is metaphoric.

thoughts and passions from a genuine cause, the inventions from a delicate feeling. This foundation of the poem, its significance, shall form the transition between the expression, that which is presented, the sensuous subject matter, that which is actually pronounced in the poem, and between the spirit, the idealistic treatment. The significance of the poem can have a twofold meaning, just as the spirit, the ideal, as well as the subject matter, the presentation, have a twofold meaning, namely, insofar as it is understood as applied or unapplied. Unapplied, these words designate nothing but the poetic operation as it can be observed [to be] genial and guided by judgment in any genuinely-poetic operation; applied, those words designate the appropriateness of the respective poetic sphere[3] of influence for that poetic operation, the possibility, which lies in the element, to realize that operation, so that one can say: in the respective element, the ideal, life [and] the individual each oppose themselves in an objective and authentic manner,[4] and one only wonders what is to be understood by this sphere of influence. It is that within which and in relation to which the respective poetic transaction and operation is realized, the vehicle of the spirit by means of which the spirit reproduces itself within itself and others. *In* itself the sphere of influence is larger than the poetic spirit, yet not *of* itself. Insofar as it | is considered in relation to the world, it is larger; insofar as it is held fast and appropriated by the poet, it is subordinated. In its tendency, the content of its striving, it is opposed to the poetic transaction, and the poet is misled all too easily by his subject matter in that the latter, removed from the interrelation with the living world, resists the poetic restriction, in that it will not merely serve the spirit as a vehicle; in that, even if it is chosen properly, what is the closest and next step forward for the spirit proves an obstacle and a spur with respect to poetic realization, so that its second progress must remain partially fulfilled, partially unfulfilled, p.p.

. However, it must become apparent, regardless of this conflict which the poetic spirit has in its transactions with the respective element and sphere of influence, how the former favors the latter, and how that conflict is resolved, how in the element which the poet chooses as a vehicle there nevertheless lies a receptivity for the poetic transaction, and how he realizes within

V,245

himself all postulates, the entire poetic operation in its metaphoric, its hyperbolic, and its [. . .] character in mutual effect
with the element which resists in its initial tendency and is
veritably opposed, to be sure, yet which unites with the former
in the middle point.

Between the expression (the presentation) and the free
idealistic treatment, there lies the foundation and significance
of the poem. This is what lends the poem its seriousness, its
firmness, its truth; it protects the poem [by assuring] that the
free idealistic treatment become not an empty affectation, and
that presentation become not vanity. It is the spiritual-sensuous,
the formal-material of the poem; and if the idealistic treatment
is more unifying in its metaphor, its transition [and] its episodes,
whereas its expression, the presentation in its characters, their
passions, their individualities, are more separating, then the
significance[5] rests between the two; it is characterized by being
IV,246   everywhere | opposed to itself: that—instead of the spirit com-
paring everything that is opposed in form—it separates all that
is united, fixates everything free, universalizes everything particular, because it considers what is treated not merely an individual whole, nor as an entity complemented as a whole by what
is harmoniously opposed to it, but a whole altogether, and because
the connection with what is harmoniously opposed is also possible
through something that is opposed with respect to the individual
tendency but not with respect to form; that it unites by way of
opposing, through the meeting of the extremes insofar as these
are not comparable with respect to content but with respect to
direction and degree of opposition, such that it also compares
what is most contradictory, and [that it] is quite hyperbolic, that
it does not proceed by way of opposition in form where, indeed,
the first is related to the second in content, but through opposition in content where the first is identical with the second in
form, so that naive, heroic, and ideal tendencies contradict
each other in the object of their tendency yet are comparable
in the form of their opposition and striving, and are united according to the law of activity, thus united in the most universal,
in life.

Thus, through this hyperbolic operation according to which
the idealistic, harmoniously opposed and connected, is not merely

considered as such, as beautiful life but also as life in general, hence also as capable of a different condition, and not of another harmoniously opposed one, to be sure, but of a directly opposed one, a most extreme, such that this new condition is comparable with the previous one only through the idea of life in general,— precisely through that does the poet provide the idealistic with a beginning, a direction, a significance. What is idealistic in this form is the subjective foundation of the poem, the point of departure and return, and since the inner ideal life can be understood in various modes, as life in general, as something capable of universalization, as something determinable, as something divisible, there are also various forms of subjective foundation; either the ideal mood is understood as feeling; | then it is the subjective foundation of the poem, the principal mood of the poet for the entire operation, and because it is held fast as feeling, by virtue of its being founded, it is held to be capable of universalization,— or it is determined ás a striving; then it becomes the principal mood of the poet for the entire operation; and that it is determined as striving causes it to be considered capable of being fulfilled by virtue of being founded; or if it is fixed as intellectual intuition, then this is the basic mode of the poet throughout the entire operation; and that it has been fixed as such causes it to be looked at as something capable of realization. And thus the subjective foundation demands, determines and prepares an objective one. In the first case, then, the subject matter is first conceived of as something universal, in the second as something fulfilling, in the third as something that happens.

V,247

Once the free, ideal, poetic life is thus fixated, and once— depending on how it was defined—it has received its significance, as capable of universalization, fulfillment, realization, once it is in this manner connected with its diametrical opposite and conceived of hyperbolically, through the idea of life in general, then the operation of the poetic spirit lacks one more important point by way of which it affords its operation not the mood, the tone, nor the significance and direction but the reality.

For if considered as pure poetic life, poetic life with respect to its content remains—as something that is, by virtue of the harmonious in general and due to temporal deficiency, connected with the harmoniously opposed—essentially unified; and it is only opposed in the alternation of forms, only with regard to the manner not the foundation of its striving; it is only more flexible, more focused, cast, interrupted to some extent only by accident; considered as life determined and founded by the poetic reflection which is based on the idea of life in general and the lack in unity, it opens in an idealistic, characteristic mood; it is now no longer something generally connected with what is harmoniously

IV,248   opposed, it exists as such in definite form | and progresses through the alternation of moods where each time the succeeding mood is determined by the preceding one and—as regards contents, that is, the organs by which it is comprised—is more opposed and hence more individual, universal, and full; so that the various modes are connected only there wherein the pure finds its opposition, namely, in the manner of striving, as life in general, such that the purely poetic life is no longer to be found, for in each of the changing moods it is connected in particular form with what hence is directly opposed to it [and] what hence is no longer pure; on the whole, it exists only as something striving, and according to the law of striving only as life, and in this respect there exists indeed a conflict between what is individual (material), universal (formal) and pure.

The pure [which is] comprised in every particular mode conflicts with the organ by which it is comprised, conflicts with the pure of the other organ, conflicts with the alternation.

As a particular organ (form), as characteristic mood, the universal conflicts with the pure which it comprises in this mood; overall it conflicts as striving with the pure which it comprises, it conflicts as the characteristic mood with the one that is closest to it.

The individual conflicts with the pure which it comprises, it conflicts with the closest form, it conflicts as individual with the universality of the alternation.

Hence the mode of operation of the poetic spirit in its workings cannot possibly end here. If it is the authentic one, then there must be something else detectable in it, and it has to become apparent that the operation which gives the poem its significance, is merely the transition from the pure to what is to be detected as well as backward from the latter to the pure. (Medium of transition beween spirit and sign.)

,249   Now, if what is directly opposed to the spirit, the organ by which the spirit is comprised and by means of which all opposition is made possible, | could be looked at and understood not only as that by which the harmoniously connected is opposed in form, but also [as that] by which it is connected in form, if it could be looked at and understood not only as that by which the various unharmonious moods are materially opposed and connected in form, but also [as that] by which they are connected in material and opposed in form, if it could be looked at and understood not only as that which, as connecting merely formal life and as particular and material one not connecting but only opposing and separating, if it could be looked at as material, as connecting, if the organ of the spirit could be looked at as that which, in order to make possible the harmoniously opposed, must be *receptive*—for the one as well as for the other harmoniously opposed—so that, to the extent that it is a formal opposition for the pure poetic life, it must also be formal connection, that, insofar as it is materially opposing for the fixed poetic life and its moods, it must also be materially connecting, that what defines and determines is not only negative, that it is also positive, that, if considered in isolation with what is harmoniously connected, it is opposed to the one as well as to the other, yet [is] the union of the two, if both are considered simultaneously, then that act of the spirit which, as regards the significance, entailed only a continuous conflict, will be as much a uniting one as it was an opposing one.

Yet how is it [the act of the spirit] comprehended within this quality? as possible and as necessary? Not merely through life in general, for it is life to the extent that it is considered merely as materially opposing and formally connecting, as directly determining life. Nor merely through the unity in general, for the spirit determines life insofar as it is merely conceived of as formally opposing, yet in the concept of the unity of that which is unified, so that of the harmoniously connected there exists at the point of opposition and unification one as well as the other, and that *at this point the spirit*, which appeared as finite by virtue of the opposition, | is *tangible in its infinity*; that the pure, conflicting as such with the organ, is present to itself in this very organ and only thus becomes a living one; that where it is present

,250

in different moods, the one following the basic tone is only the prolonged point which leads there, namely, to the center point where the harmoniously opposed modes meet one another, so that precisely in the strongest opposition, in the opposition of the first, ideal and the second, artificially reflected mood, in the most material opposition, (which lies between harmoniously connected spirit and life, which meet and are present at the center point), that precisely in this most material opposition which opposes itself (with respect to the point of union toward which it strives) in the conflicting, onward-striving acts of the spirit— if they only emerge from the reciprocal character of the harmoniously opposed modes—that precisely there the most infinite presents itself in the most tangible, most negative-positive and hyperbolical manner; that through this opposition of the presentation of the infinite in the conflicting striving toward the point and its coinciding at the point, the simultaneous inwardness and differentiation of the harmoniously opposed, living [and] founding sentiment is replaced and at the same time is presented more distinctly and more formed, more universal, as [an] autonomous world with respect to form, as [a] world within the world, and thus as voice of the eternal directed to the eternal by the free consciousness.

Thus the poetic spirit cannot content itself with the operation to which it adheres during its transaction, in a harmoniously opposed life, nor with conceiving of and holding fast the same by way of hyperbolical opposition; once it is so advanced, once its transactions lack neither harmonious unity nor significance and energy, neither harmonious spirit in general nor harmonious alternation, then it is necessary—if the unified (to the extent | that it can be considered by itself) shall not cancel itself as something undifferentiable and become an empty infinity, or if it shall not lose its identity in an alternation of opposites, however harmonious they may be, thus be no longer anything integral and unified, but shall disintegrate into an infinity of isolated moments (a sequence of atoms, as it were)—I say: then it is necessary that the poetic spirit in its unity and harmonious progress also provide for itself an infinite perspective for its transaction, a unity where in the harmonious progress and alternation everything move forward and backward and, through its sustained

IV,251

characteristic relation to that unity, not only gain objective
coherence for the observer [but] also gain [a] felt and tangible
coherence and identity in the alternation of oppositions; and it
is its last task, to have a thread, to have a recollection so that
the spirit remain present to itself never in the individual moment
and again in an individual moment, but continue in one moment
as in another and in the different moods, just as it is entirely
present to itself *in the infinite unity* which is once the point of
separation for the unified as such, but then again also point of
union for the unified as the opposed, finally is also both at once,
so that what is harmoniously opposed within it is neither opposed
as something unified nor unified as something opposed but as
both in One, is felt as opposed in unified manner as inseparable
and is invented as something felt. This sense is veritably poetical
character, neither genius nor art, but poetic individuality, and
it alone is given the identity of enthusiasm, the perfection of
genius and art, the actualization of the infinite, the divine
moment.

It[6] is therefore never the mere opposition of what is unified,
nor [is it] ever the mere relation [or] unification of the opposing
and changing; what is opposed and unified is inseparable within
it. If this is the case, then—as original sense—it can be passive
in its purity and subjective wholeness, in the acts of opposing
and unifying, to be sure, | yet in its last act, where the harmo-
niously opposed as the harmonious which is opposed, the unified
as reciprocal effect are enclosed within it as one, in this act it
simply cannot and must not be understood through itself, nor
become its own object if, instead of an infinite, unified and living
unity, there shall not exist a dead and deadly unity, something
that has become infinitely positive; for if within it unity and
opposition are inseparably linked and one, then it can appear to
reflection neither as an opposable unity nor as a unifiable opposition, thus cannot appear at all or only in the character of a
positive nothing, an infinite stagnation, and it is the hyperbole
of all hyperboles, the boldest and ultimate attempt of the poetic
spirit—if it ever undertakes it in its operation—to assess the
original poetic individuality, the poetic "I," an attempt through
which it would supercede this individuality and its pure object,
the unified and live, harmonious, mutually effective life, and yet

',252

it needs to make it; for since it shall and must be everything that its operations involve with *freedom*, insofar as it creates a proper world and the instinct naturally belongs to the actual world in which it exists, since it shall be everything with freedom, it, too, must assure itself of its individuality. However, since the poetic spirit cannot know the world in itself nor of itself, an external object is necessary, and indeed such through which the individuality, among several neither merely opposing nor merely relating but poetic characters which it can assume, be determined to assume some specific one; so that the individuality and its character now chosen, determined by the now chosen subject matter, can be recognized and fixated with freedom in the pure individuality as well as in the other characters.

(Within the subjective nature the 'I' can only form knowledge as an opposing or relating one; however, within the subjective nature it cannot recognize itself as poetic 'I' in a threefold

IV,253 | quality; for given the way in which appears within the subjective nature and is differentiated from itself and by and through itself, that which is cognized[7] must always constitute that threefold nature of the poetic 'I' together with the cognizing and the cognition of both, and must be grasped neither as cognized by the cognizing ['I'], nor as cognizing by the cognizing [itself], nor as the cognized and cognizing by cognition, nor as cognition by the cognizing; in none of these three distinctly considered qualities is it conceived of as pure poetic 'I' in its threefold nature: as opposing the harmoniously opposed, as (formally) uniting the harmoniously opposed, as comprehending in one the harmonious opposed, the opposition and unification; on the contrary, it remains in real contradiction with and for itself.* Thus only to

---

*It is simply not conceivable for itself in its real conflict as something materially opposed (for a third one but not for itself) thus as something formally uniting (as something cognized), as something opposing, thus (for a third) formally united, as something cognizing; as something opposed, formally uniting, as something opposing, formally united in cognition, opposed in what is materially united and opposed, hence [. . .]

To the extent that the 'I' in its subjective nature differs from itself and posits itself as opposing unity in the harmoniously opposed, insofar as this is harmonious or [exists] as unifying unity within the harmoniously opposed,

V,254   the extent that it is not differentiated from itself and by and |
through itself, if it is rendered distinctly differentiable by a third
part, and if this third part, insofar as it was chosen with freedom,
also insofar as it does not cancel the pure individuality with its
influence and determinations but can be looked at from the latter,

---

insofar as this is opposed, then, it must deny either the reality of the opposition,
[that is] of the difference through which it forms knowledge itself, and it must
declare the differentiating within the subjective nature either a deception and
volition which it produces for itself as unity in order to know its identity; then
the identity, too, as | something thus understood is a deception; the subjective
nature does not know itself or it is not unity, takes the difference from itself
for (dogmatically) real, namely, that the "I" act as that which differentiates or
unifies respectively, depending on whether, in its subjective nature, it finds
something to be differentiated or unified; it therefore posits itself as something
differentiating and unifying in dependence, and—because this is supposed to
occur within its subjective nature from which it cannot abstract without
superceding itself—absolutely dependent in its acts, so that it knows *itself*, *its*
act, neither as something opposing nor as something unifying. In this case it
once again cannot recognize itself as identical, because the different acts in
which it exists are not *its* acts; it cannot even posit itself as something comprehended within these acts, for these acts do not depend on it; not the 'I' is
what differs from itself but its nature in which it acts in such manner as
something driven.

However, even if the 'I' wanted to posit itself as identical with the
harmoniously opposed of its nature (to cut with the sword through the contradiction between art and genius, freedom and organic necessity, this eternal
knot), nothing would help; for if the difference between the opposing and
uniting is not a real one, then neither the 'I' can be discerned within its
harmoniously opposed life, nor the harmoniously opposed life within the 'I' as
unity; if it is real, then again neither the 'I' is discernible in what is harmoniously
opposed as unity through itself, for it is something driven, nor is the harmon-
iouslyopposed as unity discernible in its 'I', for as something driven this one is
not discernible as unity.

What everything depends on, then, is that the 'I' remain not merely in
reciprocal activity with its subjective nature, from which it cannot abstract
without superceding itself, but that it freely choose an object from which, if
it wants, it can abstract without cancelling itself in order to be adequately
determined by it and determine it.

Herein rests the possibility that the 'I' become discernible in the harmoniously opposed life as unity, and that the harmoniously opposed become
discernible in the 'I' as unity in pure, (poetic), individuality. Pure life is led
to free individuality, unity and identity within itself only through the choice
of its object.

IV,255   where it thus simultaneously conceives of itself | as something determined by choice, something empirically individualized and characterized, only then is it possible that the 'I' appear as unity in the harmoniously opposed life and, conversely, that what is harmoniously opposed appear as unity in the 'I' and become object in beautiful individuality.)

(a) Yet how is it possible? universally?

(b) Once it becomes possible in such a manner that the 'I' recognizes and conducts itself in poetic individuality, what results from that for poetic presentation? (It recognizes within the three subjective and objective attempts the striving for pure unity.)

(a) If man has lived in this solitude, in this life with himself, this contradictory middle-stage between the natural relationship with a naturally present world and the higher relationship with an also naturally present world, yet one which is in advance freely elected and recognized as the sphere and determining him with all its influences yet not without his will, once he has lived in that middle-state between childhood and mature humanity, between what is mechanically beautiful and what is humanely beautiful, in that life beautiful with freedom, and has recognized and experienced this middle-state, as indeed he has to remain inevitably in contradiction with himself, within the necessary conflict (1) of the striving for pure selfhood and identity, (2) of the striving for significance [*Bedeutenheit*] and differentiation, (3) of the striving for harmony, and how in this struggle each of these aspirations has to cancel itself and show itself as unrealizable, how he therefore must resignate, fall back into childhood or exhaust himself in fruitless contradictions with himself: if he remains in this state, then there is one thing that will draw him out of this sad alternative; and the problem to be free like a youth, and to live in the world like a child, the problem of the independence of a cultivated being and of the accomodation of an ordinary being is solved by following the rule:

IV,256   Posit yourself by *free choice* into a harmonious opposition | with an outer sphere just as by nature you are in harmonious opposition with yourself, yet unrecognizably so, as long as you remain within yourself.

For here, by following this rule, there exists an important difference regarding the behavior in the previous state.

In the previous state, namely, in that of solitude, the harmoniously opposed nature could not become a recognizable unity
because the 'I,' without cancelling itself, could neither posit and
recognize itself as active unity without cancelling the reality of
the distinction and thus the reality of the act of cognition, nor
[could posit itself] as suffering unity without cancelling the reality
of the unity, its criterion of identity, namely, activity; and that
the 'I,' striving to recognize its unity in that which is harmoniously opposed and to recognize what is harmoniously opposed
within its unity, that the 'I' must posit itself in such absolute
and dogmatic manner as active unity, or as suffering unity, happens because, in order to recognize itself through itself, it can
replace the naturally close connection which it has with itself,
and due to which the differentiation is made difficult for it, only
with an unnatural (self-cancelling) distinction; because, in its
difference from itself, it is thus by nature one, that the difference
necessary for cognition, which it gives to itself through freedom,
is only possible in extremes, thus only in striving, in thought-
experiments which, if realized in this manner, would cancel
themselves because, in order to recognize its unity in the (subjective) harmoniously opposed and [to recognize] the (subjective)
harmoniously opposed in its unity, it must necessarily abstract
from itself insofar as it is posited in the (subjective) harmoniously
opposed, and must reflect upon itself insofar as it is not posited
in the (subjective) harmoniously opposed, and vice versa; however, since it can neither produce these abstractions from its
being in the (subjective) harmoniously opposed, nor this reflection on non-being without cancelling itself and the harmoniously
opposed, without cancelling the subjective, harmonious and
I,257   opposed and the unity, so | the experiments which it nevertheless
undertakes in this manner must also be such that, if realized in
this manner, they would cancel themselves.

This, then, is the difference between the state of solitude
(the intuition of its essence)[8] and the new state where man posits
himself freely in harmonious opposition with an outer sphere
that, precisely because he is *not* so intimately connected with it,
he can abstract from it and can abstract from himself insofar as
he *is* posited in it, and [that he] can reflect upon himself insofar
as he is not posited in it; this is the reason why he moves beyond

himself, this the rule for his mode of operation in the outer world. In this manner he reaches his destiny which is—knowledge of what is harmoniously opposed within him, within his unity and individuality, and then again knowledge of his identity, his unity and individuality within the harmoniously opposed. This is the true freedom of his being, and if he does not adhere too much to this exterior, harmoniously opposed sphere, does not become identical with it as with himself, so that he can never abstract from it, nor adheres too much to himself and can abstract too little from himself as someone independent, if he neither reflects too much upon himself nor reflects too much upon his sphere and epoch, then he is on the right way of his destination [*Bestimmung*]. The childhood of the ordinary life when he was identical with the world and unable to abstract from it, when he was without freedom, hence without knowledge of himself within the harmoniously opposed nor of the harmoniously opposed within himself, in fact, without firmness, autonomy, actual identity in pure life, this time will be considered by him the time of wishes where man strives to recognize himself within the harmoniously opposed and the latter within himself as unity, in that he devotes himself altogether to the objective life; yet there the impossibility of a recognizable identity becomes manifest within the harmoniously opposed in an objective manner as it has already been demonstrated in a subjective manner. For since in this state

IV,258   he does not have any knowledge whatsoever | of his subjective nature, since he is merely objective life within the objective, he can thus only strive to recognize the unity in the harmoniously opposed by proceeding within his sphere, from which he can abstract as little as the subjective man can from his own, as the latter does within his sphere. He is posited in it as within the harmoniously opposed. He must strive to recognize himself, must attempt to differentiate himself from himself within it by positing himself as the opposing [principle] insofar as it is harmonious, and as the unifying [principle] insofar as it is opposed. Yet if he strives to recognize himself within this difference, then he must either deny the reality of the opposition in which he exists with himself and must consider this opposing procedure as an illusion and something arbitrary which becomes only manifest so that he recognize his identity in the harmoniously opposed—yet then this identity of his as something recognized is also an illusion—

or he considers this distinction something real, namely, that he
conduct himself as something unifying or differentiating depending on whether he find within his sphere something to be differentiated or to be united, thus positing himself as something
unifying and differentiating with dependency, because this is
supposed to happen within his objective sphere from which he
cannot abstract without cancelling himself, with absolute
dependency, so that he recognizes *his act for himself* neither as
something unifying nor as something opposing. In this case, he
once again cannot recognize himself as identical, because the
different acts wherein he finds himself are not his acts. He cannot
recognize himself, he is nothing differentiable; it is his sphere
wherein he behaves so mechanically. Yet, even if he wished to
posit himself as identical with this [sphere], to dissolve in highest
inwardness the conflict between life and personality which he
always strives and must strive to unify and recognize within one,
then it is to no avail, insofar as he behaves within his sphere
insuch a manner that he cannot abstract from it; for because he
lives too intensely in his sphere, he can recognize himself only
in extreme oppositions of differentiation and unification.

IV,259 | Thus man, in a too subjective as well as in a too objective
state, seeks in vain to reach his destiny which consists in that
he recognize himself as a unity contained within the divine—
harmoniously opposed and, vice versa, the divine, unified, harmonious opposed within himself as unity. For this is possible only
in beautiful, sacred, divine sentiment, in a sentiment which is
beautiful because it is neither merely pleasant and happy, nor
merely sublime and powerful, nor merely unified and tranquil,
but is everything at once and can exist for itself, in a sentiment
which is sacred because it is neither merely selflessly devoted to
its object nor merely resting selflessly on its inner foundations,
nor merely hovering between its inner foundation and its object,
but is everything at once and can exist for itself; in a sentiment
which is divine because it is neither mere consciousness, mere
reflection (subjective or objective) with the loss of the inner and
outer life, nor mere striving (subjectively or objectively determined) with the loss of the inner and outer harmony, nor mere
harmony like the intellectual intuition and its mythical, figur-
ative subject, object, with the loss of the consciousness and the
unity; but because it is all this at once and can exist for itself,

in a sentiment which is transcendental and can be so for itself, because in the unification and reciprocal effect of the charac-teristics named above, it is neither too pleasant and sensuous, nor too energetic and wild, nor too intimate and enthusiastic, nor too selfless, that is, devoted to its object in a too self-forgetful manner, nor too unselfish, that is, resting on its inner foundation in a too autocratic manner, nor too selfish, that is, hovering between its inner foundation and its object in a too undecided, empty and indetermined manner; neither too reflected, too con-scious of itself, too acute and therefore unconscious of its inner and outer foundation, nor too moved and too much caught in its inner and outer foundation, precisely therefore unconscious of the harmony of the inner and the outer, nor too harmonious,

IV,260   therefore too little conscious of itself and of the inner | and outer foundation, therefore too undetermined and less receptive to the properly infinite which is defined by it as a determined, authentic infinity, located in the exterior. In short, because it exists in a threefold characteristic and can do so for itself; it is less exposed to a bias in any one of the three characteristics. On the contrary, there originally arise from it all the forces which possess those characteristics in more determined and recognizable manner, to be sure, yet also in a more isolated manner, just as those forces and their characteristics and manifestations again concentrate and gain within it—through mutual coherence and through liv-ing, independently existing determinacy, as organs of it—freedom as belonging to it and something not restricted to itself in its limitedness and completeness as comprised in its totality; those three characteristics, as striving to recognize the harmonious opposed in the living unity or vice versa, may find expression in the more subjective or objective state. For precisely these states also emerge from it as the unification of the former ones.

$$S [\ldots]^9$$

Suggestion for Presentation and Language

Is not language like the cognition that was mentioned before and about which it was said that as a unity it contained the unified and vice versa? and that it be of a threefold kind p.p.

Must not, for the one as well as for the other, the most beautiful moment rest where there lies the actual expression, the most intellectual language, the most vivid consciousness, the transition from a specific infinity to a more universal one?

IV,261

|Does not the stable point lie precisely there whereby the mode of relation is determined for the sequence of the portrayal, and where the character and degree [are determined] for the local colors as well as for the illumination?

Will not all qualification of language be reduced to one'a examining—according to the *most certain and possibly least misleading features*—whether it be the language of an authentic, beautifully described sensation?

Just as cognition intuits language, so does language remember cognition.

Cognition intuits language after it 1) was yet unreflected pure sentiment of life, of the specific infinity by which it is contained, 2) after it had repeated itself in the dissonances of the internal reflecting, striving and poeticizing and now, after these futile attempts to recover and reproduce itself internally, after these silent intuitions which, too, need their time, moves beyond itself and recovers itself in the entire infinity, that is, which—through the immaterial, pure mode, virtually through the resonance of the primordial, living sensation which it gained and could gain, through the complete effect of all internal attempts, through this higher divine receptivity—masters and internalizes its complete outer and inner life. At precisely this moment when the primordeal, living sensation which has been purified into the pure mood that is receptive to something infinite, exists as infinite within the infinite, as an intellectual whole within a living whole, it is at this moment that one can say that language is intuited; and if now a reflection occurs, as in the primordial sensation, then it is no longer dissolving and universalizing, disseminating and form-giving to the point of mere mood; it restores to the heart everything that it took away from it; it is enlivening art as it was intellectualizing art before, and with one stroke of magic after another it invokes the lost life all the more beautifully until it feels once again entirely as it used

IV,262

to feel originally. And if it is the course and the | destiny of life in general[10] to develop from the primordeal simplicity to the highest form where, precisely for that reason, the infinite life is present to man, and where he receives what is most abstract all the more intensely in order to then reissue—out of this highest opposition and unification of the living and the intellectual, of the formal and material subject-object—for the spirit its life, for life its form, for man his sympathy and his heart, and for his world the gratitude, and finally, after fulfilled intuition and hope— namely, if in the expression there existed that highest point of cultivation, the highest form in the highest life and where, not only with itself, as in the beginning of the actual expression, nor in the striving where, like in the ongoing of the same, the expression evokes life out of the spirit and spirit out of life, but where it has found the primordial life in the highest form; where spirit and life are equal on both sides and recognize the find [of expression], the infinite within the infinite after this third and last completion, which is not merely primordial simplicity of the heart and of life where man feels himself uninhibitedly as in a restricted infinity, nor merely attained simplicity of the spirit where that very sensation which is purified to a pure [and] formal mood receives the entire infinity of life, (and is ideal), but which is instead spirit reanimated by the infinite life, not chance, not ideal, but is accomplished work and creation, and which is only found in expression, and which, outside of expression, can only be hoped for in the ideal that emerged from its determined, primordial sensation—how finally, after this third completion, where the determined infinity has been called into life so far, where the infinite one is intellectualized so much that one equals the other in spirit and life, how after this third completion that which is determined is increasingly animated, the infinite is increasingly intellectualized, until the primordial sensation fin- ishes as life just as it set out as spirit in the expression, and until

IV,263   the higher infinity from which it took its life | becomes intel- lectualized just as it existed as something living in the expression,—

hence, if this appears to be the course and the destination of man in general, then the very same thing is the course and the destiny of all and any poesy; and just as on any level of cultivation where man, having emerged from primordial childhood, has struggled in opposed efforts to the highest of forms, to the pure resonance of the primordial life and thus feels himself as infinite spirit in the infinite life, just as man only begins life and intuits his impact and destiny on this level of cultivation, so the poet intuits, at that level where he too, out of a primordial sensation, has struggled in opposed efforts to the tone, to the highest, pure form of the same sensation and where he conceives of himself as altogether comprehended in his entire inner and outer life by that tone; on that level he intuits his language and along with it the actual perfection for the present and simultaneously for all poesy.

It has already been said that on that level there enters a reflection which restores everything to the heart that it had taken from it, which is enlivening art for the spirit of the poet and his future poem, just as it had been intellectualizing art for the primordial sensation of the poet and his poem. *The product of this creative reflection is language.* Namely, in that the poet feels himself comprehended in his entire inner and outer life by the pure tone of his primordial sensation and looks around in his world this is as new and unfamiliar to him; the sum of all his experiences, of his knowledge, of his intuition, of his thinking, art and nature, as they present themselves within him and outside of him, everything exists, as it were, for the first time and for that reason is uncomprehended, undetermined, dissolved into pure matter and life, present to him; and it is especially important that at this moment he takes nothing for granted, proceeds from nothing positive, that nature and art, as he has come to know them and sees them, speak not until there | exists a language for him, that is, until what is now unknown and unnamed in his world becomes known and named precisely by way of having been compared and found in congruence with his mood; for if, prior to the reflection on the infinite subject matter and the infinite form, there existed for him some language of nature and art in specific form, then he would to that extent not be in his sphere of effect; he would step outside of his creation, and the language of nature or art, every *modus exprimendi* of the one or the other—insofar as it is not *his* language, not a product which emerged from his life and from his spirit, but as language of art— as soon as it is present to me in determined form, would already be a seriously determining act of the artist's creative reflection which consisted in that, out of his world, out of the sum of his outer and inner life which is also more or less mine, that out of this world he took the subject matter in order to designate the tones of his spirit, to evoke out of this mood the fundamental life through this related sign; thus that he, insofar as he names for me this sign, as he borrows the subject matter from my world, as he causes me to transfer this subject matter into the sign where, then, that important difference exists between me as the determined and him as the determining one; that, by making himself comprehensible and tangible he moves away from the lifeless, immaterial, hence less opposable and less conscious mood precisely by explaining (1) its infinity of agreement through a totality of related subject matter, relative in form and substance, and through an ideally transforming world, (2) its determination and actual finiteness through the presentation and enumeration of its own subject matter, (3) its tendency, its universality in the particular through the opposition between its own and the infinite subject matter, (4) its proportion in the beautiful determination, unity and firmness of its infinite agreement, its infinite

IV,265 identity, individuality and attitude, | its poetic prose of an all-delimiting moment whereto and wherein all named parts refer and unite in a negative and therefore explicit and sensuous manner; namely, [he explains] the infinite form with the infinite subject matter in that through that moment the infinite form assumes a configuration, the alternation of the weaker and the stronger, that the infinite subject matter assumes a pleasant resonance, an alternation of the brighter and quieter, and that the two, in the retardation and accelleration, are eventually negatively united in the standstill of the movement, always through him [the poet] and his founding activity, through the infinite, beautiful reflection which, in the sustained delimitation, is at once continuously relating and unifying.

On the Difference of Poetic Modes[1]

The lyric, in appearance idealistic poem, is naive in its significance. It is a continuous metaphor of a feeling.

The epic, in appearance naive poem, is heroic in its significance. It is the metaphor of great aspirations.

The tragic, in appearance heroic poem, is idealistic in its significance. It is the metaphor of an intellectual intuition.

In its *basic mood*, the lyric poem is the *more sensuous*, in that this [basic mood] contains a unity which lends itself most easily; precisely for that reason does it not strive in the outer appearance for reality, serenity and gracefulness; it evades the sensuous connection and presentation so much (because the pure basic tone inclines precisely toward it) that it is rather miraculous and supernatural in its formations and assembly of these,[2] and the heroic energetic dissonances wherein it neither looses its reality, its life, as in the idealistic image, nor its tendency toward ennoblement as in the immediate expression, these energetic dissonances that unite ennoblement and life are the resolution of the contradiction at which it [the lyric poem] arrives when, on the one hand, it can and will not fall into the sensuous, nor, on the other hand, deny its basic tone, the intimate life. However, if its basic tone is more heroic, richer in content, as for instance in a Pindaric hymn to the fencer Diagoras,[3] if it therefore has to lose less inwardness, then it starts out naive; if it is more idealistic, more akin to the art-character, to the improper tone, if it has less life to lose, then it starts out heroic; if it is most inward, having content to lose, yet even more, ennoblement, purity of content, then it starts out idealistic.

| In lyric poems the emphasis is placed on the more immediate language of sentiment, on the most inward, on the repose, the stance, on the heroic, the tendency toward the idealistic.

The epic, in its outer appearance *naive poem*, is in its *basic tone* the *more pathetic*, heroic, aorgic one;[4] hence it strives in its art-character not for energy, movement and life, but for precision, calmness and pictorial quality. The opposition between its basic tone and its art-character, between its proper and its improper, metaphorical tone is resolved in the idealistic where it neither loses so much life as in its narrowly delimiting art-character nor as much moderation as in the immediate expression of its basic tone. If its basic tone, which may well be of different disposition, is more idealistic, if it has less life to lose but has a greater tendency toward organization, wholeness, then the poem may start out with its basic tone, the heroic one, *menin aeide thea*—and be heroic-epical.[5] If the basic tone has less idealistic quality yet more relation to the art-character, which is the naive one, then it starts out idealistic; if the basic tone possesses its actual character so much that it therefore must lose in idealistic quality, even more in naive quality, then it starts out as naive. If that which unites and negotiates the basic tone and the art-character of a poem is the spirit of the poem, if that one has to be sustained most, and if in the epic poem the spirit is the idealistic, then the epic poem has to remain mostly with the latter, whereas most emphasis is placed on the basic tone, which here is the energetic one, and direction [is given to] the art-character as the naive, wherein everything has to concentrate and thereby to distinguish and individualize itself.

The tragic, in its *outer appearance heroic poem* is in its *basic tone idealistic*, and all works of this kind must be founded on an intellectual intuition which cannot be any other one than that unity with everything living which, | to be sure, is not felt by the limited soul, only anticipated in its [the soul's] highest aspirations, yet which can be recognized by the spirit; it results from the impossibility of an absolute separation and individuation and is stated most easily if one says that the true separation, and with it everything truly material [and] perishable and thus, too, the union and with it all that is spiritually permanent, the objective as such and thus also the subjective as such, that they are only a state of the primordially united, a state wherein it exists because it had to transcend itself due to the stasis which could not occur in it because its mode of union could not always stay the same with regard to matter, because parts of the united must not always remain in the same closer and remoter relation, so that everything may encounter everything else and that all receive its full right and share of life, and that every part during its course equal the whole in completeness; conversely, that the whole during its course become equal to the parts in determinacy, that the former gain in content [and] the latter in inwardness; that the former gain in life, the latter ones in liveliness; that the former feel itself more in its progress, and the latter ones fulfill themselves more in progress; for it is an eternal law that the substantial whole does not feel itself in its unity with the determination and liveliness, not in that sensuous unity in which its parts—also being a whole, only more freely united—feel themselves; so that one may say: if the liveliness, determinacy [and] unity of the parts where their wholeness is felt, transcends the boundary *of the parts* and turns into suffering and, *conceivably*, into absolute determinacy and individuation, only then would the whole feel itself in *these parts* as lively and determinately as they feel themselves in a calmer yet also moved state, in their more restricted wholeness. (As is, the case, for instance, with the lyric (more individual) mood where the individual world, in its most complete existence and purest unity, strives to dissolve and seems to perish at that point where it individualizes itself, in that part where its own parts fuse, in the most intimate sentiment; how

V,269   only there the individual world senses itself in its | totality; how only there where the feeling and what is felt want to separate, the more individual unity is present and resounds most vitally and determined). Hence the tangibility of the whole progresses precisely to that extent and in that proportion with which the separation itself proceeds within the parts and in their center, wherein the parts and the whole are most tangible. The unity present in the intellectual intuition manifests itself as a sensuous one precisely to the extent that it transcends itself, that the separation of its parts occurs which, too, separate only because they feel too unified: either when, within the whole, they are closer to the centerpoint; or, when they are ancillaries, because they do not feel sufficiently unified as regards completeness, more removed from the centerpoint; or, as regards liveliness, if they are neither ancillaries nor essential parts in the above sense because they are not yet complete, but only divisible parts. And here, in the excess of spirit within unity, in its striving for materiality, in the striving of the divisible, more infinite aorgic which must contain all that is more organic—for all more determined and necessary existence requires a less determined and less necessary existence—in this striving for separation of the divisible infinite, which in the state of highest unity of everything organic imparts itself to all parts contained by this unity, in this necessary *arbitrariness of Zeus* there actually lies the ideal beginning of the real separation.

From here the separation proceeds until the parts are in their most extreme tension, where they resist one another most strongly. From this conflict, it returns into itself, namely, where the parts—at least the originally most inward ones, in their singularity as *these* parts at this place of the whole—cancel one another, and a new unity originates. The transition from the first to the second, then, is presumably that highest tension of the conflict. And the movement leading up to it differs from the return in that the former is more idealistic, the latter more real, that in the former | the motif is more ideally determining, more related to the whole than to the individual, p.p. while in the latter it has emerged more from passion and the individual.

IV,270

This basic tone is less lively than the lyric [and] more individual one. Hence, being the more universal and the most individual, it is also [. . .]

If in the basic tone of the tragic poem[6] there is more tendency to reflection and more sentiment in its balanced character, yet less tendency to presentation, less physical quality—as it is indeed natural that a poem whose significance shows more deeply and whose attitude, coherence and movement show more strongly and more gently in its most significant expressions, yet not so quickly and readily, as when the significance and the motives of expression lie closer, are more sensuous—then the tragic poem starts out accordingly with the idealistic basic tone, [. . .]

If the intellectual intuition is more subjective, and if the separation proceeds mainly from the concentrating parts, as in *Antigone*, then the style is lyrical; if it proceeds more from the ancillaries and more objective, then it is epic; if it proceeds from the highest separable, from Zeus, as in *Oedipus*, then it is tragic.

In the poem, feeling *is expressed* in an idealistic—passion in a naive—[and] fantasy in an energetic manner.

Thus once again the idealistic in the poem affects sentiment (by means of passion), the naive affects passion (by means of fantasy), the energetic affects fantasy (by means of sentiment).

| naive poem.
basic tone.
    passion. pp.   by means of fantasy.

√,271   language.
       Sentiment Passion Fantasy Sentiment Passion
               Fantasy Sentiment.
                       by means of Fantasy.
effect.
       Passion Fantasy Sentiment Passion Fantasy
           Sentiment Passion.

energetic poem.
basic tone.
 Fantasy. pp.   by means of sentiment.
 language.
         Passion Fantasy Sentiment Passion
         Fantasy Sentiment Passion.
              pref. by means of Sentiment.
effect.
        Fantasy Sentiment Passion Fantasy
        Sentiment Passion Fantasy.
idealistic poem.
basic tone.
     Sentiment, pp.   by means of passion
language.
        Fantasy Sentiment Passion Fantasy
        Sentiment Passion Fantasy.
            pref. by means of Passion.
effect.
      Sentiment Passion Fantasy Sentiment
          Passion Fantasy Sentiment.

   ?   Fantasy Passion Sentiment Fantasy

√,272 | Passion Sentiment Fantasy.
              by means of Sentiment

      Sentiment Fantasy Passion Sentiment
          Fantasy Passion Sentiment.
            Style of the song Diotima.[7]

In every poetic mode, the epic, the tragic and the lyrical, a *more substantial* basic tone will be expressed in the naive, a *more intense, sensitive* one in the idealistic, a *more spiritual* one in the energetic style; for if in the more spiritual basic tone the separation is effected by the infinite, then it has to affect first the concentrating parts or the center, it has to communicate itself to these; and insofar as the separation is a receiving one, it can express itself not as forming, not as reproducing its whole, but can only react, and this is the energetic beginning. Affected by the original separation which, however, as the more receptive one did not return it all that quickly and reacted but now, the opposed main part reacts only through the separation; through the effect and counter-effect of the main parts, the ancillaries—which also were affected by the original separation, yet only in the striving for change—are not moved to actual expression, by this expression the main parts are moved p.p., until the primordially separating has arrived at its total expression.

If the separation proceeds from the center, then this is effected either by the more receptive main part; for then the latter reproduces itself in idealistic forming, the separation divides [. . .]

The Significance of Tragedies[1]

The significance of tragedies can be understood most easily by way of paradox. Since all potential is divided justly and equally, all original matter appears not in original strength but, in fact, in its weakness, so that quite properly the light of life and the appearance attach to the weakness of every whole. Now in the tragic, the sign in itself is insignificant, without effect, yet original matter is straightforward. Properly speaking, original matter can only appear in its weakness; however, to the extent that the sign is posited as insignificant $= 0$, original matter, the hidden foundation of any nature, can also present itself. If nature properly presents itself in its weakest talent, then the sign is, nature presenting itself in its most powerful talent, $= 0$.

On Religion[1]

You ask me why, even though the people, following their nature, elevate themselves above necessity and thus exist in a more manifold and intimate relation with their world, even though, to the extent that they elevate themselves above physical and moral needs, they always live a—in human terms—higher life, so that between them and their world there be a higher [and] more than mechanical *interrelation*, a higher destiny, even though this higher relation be truly the most sacred for them because within it they themselves feel united with their world and everything which they are [and] possess, you ask me why exactly they *represent* the relation between them and their world, why they have to form an idea or image of their destiny which, strictly speaking, can neither be properly thought nor does it lie before our senses?

You ask me, and I can answer you only so much: that man also elevates himself above need in that he can *remember* his destiny, in that he can and may be grateful for his life, that he also senses more continuously his sustained relation with the element in which he moves, that by elevating himself above necessity in his efficiency and the experience connected to it, he experiences a more infinite [and] continuous satisfaction than is the satisfaction of basic needs, provided that, on the one hand, his activity is of the right kind, is not too far-reaching for him, for his strength and skill, that he is not too restless, too undetermined nor, on the other hand, too anxious, too restricted, too controlled. However, if man approaches it the right way, then there exists, in every sphere that is proper to him, a more than necessity-based, infinite satisfaction. Just as every satisfaction is a momentary standstill of *real* life, | so, too, is an infinite satisfaction, only with that great difference that the satisfaction of basic needs is followed by a negative one as, for example, animals usually sleep when they have satisfied their appetite, while infinite satisfaction is also followed by a standstill of real life yet this life occurring in the spirit, and man's power repeats in the spirit the real life which afforded him the satisfaction until the completeness and incompleteness proper to this spiritual repetition drives him again into real life. I say: that infinite, more than necessity-based relation, that higher destiny which man experiences in his element is also felt more infinitely by him, satisfies him infinitely; and out of this satisfaction there emerges the spiritual life where he, as it were, repeats his real life.[2] Yet to the extent that a higher, more infinite relation exists between him and his element in his real life, this [relation] can neither be merely repeated in *thought* nor merely in *memory*, for mere thought, however noble, can repeat only the *necessary relation*, only the inviolable, universal, indispensable laws of life; and precisely to the degree that [thought] moves beyond this proper realm and dares to think the more intrinsic relation of life, it also denies its proper character which consists in that it can be accepted and proven without particular examples; those infinite, more than necessary relations of life can be thought, to be sure, but not *merely* thought; thought does not exhaust them, and if there exist higher laws which determine that infinite relation of life, if there exist unwritten divine laws of which Antigone speaks when, in spite of the strict public interdict, she had buried her brother,—and there must be such laws if that higher relation is not enthusiasm—I say: if there are such, then they are insufficient to the extent that they are understood [and] represented only by

V,277   themselves and not in life because, to the | extent that the nexus of life becomes more infinite, the activity and its element, the mode of procedure and the sphere in which it is observed, that is, the law and the particular world in which it is enacted, interrelate more infinitely; and because the law, even if it was a universal for civilized people, could never be conceived of abstractly without a particular case unless one were to take away from it its peculiarity, its intimate relation with the sphere in which it is enacted. And still, then, the laws of that infinite relation in which man exists with his sphere are always only the conditions which make that relation possible, and not the relation itself.

Hence this higher relation cannot be merely repeated in thought. Thus one can speak of the duty of hospitality, of the duty to be generous to one's enemies, one can speak of what is and what is not appropriate for this or that way of life, for this or that rank, for this or that generation or gender, and we have indeed partially turned those more refined and infinite relations of life into vain etiquette or stale rules of taste and consider ourselves more enlightened with those adamantine terms than the ancients who regarded those tender relations as religious ones, that is, as relations which one had to look at not in and of themselves but rather from [the viewpoint of] the *spirit* that ruled the sphere in which those relations existed. (Further elaboration.) *

IV,278

And this, then, is the higher enlightenment that we are mostly lacking. Those more tender and infinite relations, then, must | be considered from the spirit that rules the sphere in which they occur. This spirit, however, this infinite relation, itself [. . .] has to keep, and to this one and nothing else does and must he refer when he speaks of a divinity, and when he speaks from the heart and not based on a helpful memory or professional considerations. The proof lies in few words. Neither solely by himself nor by means of the objects surrounding him, can man experience that more than the course of a machine, that a spirit, a god exists in the world but in a more living relation, superior to basic needs, in which he exists within his environment.

And hence everyone would have his own god to the extent that everyone has his own sphere in which he works and which he experiences, and only to the extent that several men have a common sphere in which they work and suffer humanely, that is, elevated above basic needs, only to that extent do they have a common divinity; and if there exists a sphere in which they all exist simultaneously and to which they bear a relation of more

---

*In how far were *they right?* As we already saw, they were right because—to the extent that the relations transcend the physically and morally necessary—the mode of procedure and its element, which can be thought as absolute in the form and modality of certain basic experiences, are more inseparably connected.

than basic needs, then, and only to that extent do they all have a common divinity.

However, it must not be forgotten here, that man can also put himself into the position of another one, that he can make the sphere of the other one his own, hence that it can naturally not be so difficult for one to accept the mode of feeling and IV,279 representation of the divine which emerges | from the particular relations that he bears to the world—if, on the other hand, those representations have not emerged from a passionate, presumptuous or slavish life which also always forms a likewise base, passionate representation of the spirit ruling in this life, so that this spirit always bears the appearance of the tyrant or the slave. Yet even in a restricted life man can exist infinitely, and also the limited representation of a divinity which emerges for him from his life can be an infinite one. Develop.

Hence, as someone can accept the limited yet pure way of life of the other one, he can also accept the limited yet pure representation which the other one has of the divine. On the contrary, it is a need of people, as long as they are not hurt and bothered, as long as, oppressed and rebellious, they are not engaged in just or unjust fight, to associate their various representations of the divine with one another like all other interests and thus give freedom to the limitation that each individual representation has and must have in that it is now comprehended in a harmonic whole of representational modes and—precisely because in each representation there also lies the significance of the particular way of life which everyone possesses—to simultaneously accord the necessary limitedness of this mode of life its freedom in that IV,280 it is comprehended within a harmonic whole of modes of life. | [. . .]³ and as he conceives of it more distinctly and darker in an image whose character expresses the character of the specific life which everyone can live and lives infinitely in his own way. [. . .] that is, are such where the people who exist with them, can indeed exist without one another in isolation, and that these legal conditions become effective only in the case of their disturbance, that is, that this disturbance is not an omission but a violent act and thus is inhibited and restricted once again through violence and coercion, so that also the laws of those relations are negative as such and positive only under the condition of their transgression; whereas those freer relations, as long as they are what they are, and exist undisturbed, [. . .] hints for continuation.[4]

on the one hand, the difference between religious conditions and intellectual, moral-legal conditions, on the other hand, physical, mechanical, historical conditions, so that the religious conditions have their personality, their autonomy, the reciprocal restricting, the negative, equal coexistence of intellectual conditions as well as the intrinsic coherence, one being given to the other, the inseparability in their parts which characterizes the parts of a physical relation; thus the religious conditions are neither intellectual nor historical in their *representation* but intellectually historical, that is, *mythical* regarding their subject as well as their presentation. With regard to the subject, they neither become mere ideas or concepts or characters, nor do they contain mere events, facts, nor both of these in separation, but

IV,281   both in one, and indeed in such a way that where the | personal parts have more weight, where they are [the] main parts [and] the inner content, the presentation, the external content will be more historical (epic myth), and where the event is the main part [and] inner content, the external content will be more personal (dramatic myth); yet one must not forget that the personal parts as well as the historical ones are always only ancillary parts in relation to the true main part, to the *god of the myth.* *

Thus also the presentation of the myth. On the one hand, its parts are assembled such that, due to their continuous, reciprocal, appropriate restriction, none stands forth too much, and that thereby each one achieves a certain degree of autonomy; and to that extent the presentation will bear an intellectual character. On the other hand, precisely because each part goes a little further than is necessary, they will achieve that inseparability which otherwise is only proper to the parts of a physical, mechanical relation.

Thus all religion would be poetic in its essence.

Here there can yet be spoken about the uniting of several religions into one, where each one honors his god and all together

---

*The lyric-mythical needs yet to be determined.

honor a communal one in poetic representations; where each one celebrates his higher life and all together celebrate a communal higher life, the celebration of life [as such]. Furthermore, we could talk about founders of religion, about priests, which they are if looked at from this perspective; the former ones founders of religion (if they are not fathers of a family which passes down to its heirs the occupation and the destiny of the same), if they [. . .]

Becoming in Dissolution[1]

The declining fatherland, nature and man, insofar as they bear a particular relation of reciprocity, insofar as they constitute a special world which has become ideal and [constitute] a union of things and insofar as they dissolve, so that from the world and from the remaining ancestry and forces of nature, which are the other real principle, there emerge a new world, a new yet also particular reciprocal relation just as that decline emerged from a pure yet particular world.[2] For the world of all worlds, the all in all which always *is*, only *presents* itself in all time—or in the decline, the instant or, more genetically, in the becoming of the instant and in the beginning of time and world, and this decline and beginning is—like language—expression, sign, presentation of a living yet particular whole which in its effects becomes like the former ones, namely, in such a manner, that within it—as well as in language—there seems to lie on one side less or no living existence, yet everything on the other side. In the living existence there prevails a mode of relation and of *thematics*, even though all others can be intuited within it; the possibility of all relations is predominant in the transition, yet the particular one needs to be taken, to be derived from it so that through it there emerges infinity, the finite effect.

This decline or transition of the fatherland (in this sense) is felt in the parts of the existing world so that at precisely that moment and to precisely that extent that existence dissolves, the newly-entering, the youthful, the potential is also felt. For how could dissolution be felt without union; if, then, existence shall be felt and is felt in its dissolution, then the *unexhausted* and *inexhaustible* of the *relations* and *forces* must be | felt more by dissolution than *vice versa*, for from nothing there follows nothing; and taken gradually, this means so much as that what moves toward negation, and insofar as it moves out of reality and is not yet a possibility, cannot take effect.

However, the *possible* which enters into *reality* as that *reality itself dissolves*, is operative and effects the sense of dissolution as well as the remembrance of that which has been dissolved.

Hence the thoroughly original [nature] of any truly tragic[3] language, the forever-creative . . . the genesis of the individual out of the infinite, and the originating of the finite-infinite or individual-eternal out of both, the comprehending, the animating not of what has become incomprehensible, soulless, but of the incomprehensible, soulless [quality] of the dissolution and of the struggle of death itself through the harmonic, comprehensible [and] living. In this there is not expressed the first raw pain of dissolution, still too unfamiliar in its depth for the suffering and observing man; in this, the newly-originating, the idealistic is undetermined, more an object of fear, whereas dissolution as such, an existence *per se*, seems more authentic, and the real or the dissolving is comprehended in a state of necessity between being and non-being.

The new life, which had to dissolve and did dissolve, is now truly possible (of ideal age); dissolution is necessary and holds its peculiar character between being and non-being. In the state between being and non-being, however, the possible becomes real everywhere, and the real becomes ideal, and in the free imitation of art this is a frightful yet divine dream. In the perspective of ideal recollection, then, dissolution as a necessity becomes as such the ideal object of the newly developed life, a glance back on the path that had to be taken, from the beginning of dissolution up to that moment when, in the new life, there can occur a recollection of the dissolved and thus, as explanation and union of the gap and the contrast occurring between present and past, there can occur the recollection of dissolution. This idealistic dissolution is fearless. The beginning and end | point is already posited, found, secured; and hence this dissolution is also more secure, more relentless [and] more bold, and as such it therefore presents itself as a reproductive act by means of which life runs through all its moments and, in order to achieve the total sum, stays at none but dissolves in everyone so as to constitute itself in the next; except that the dissolution becomes more ideal to the extent that it moves away from the beginning point, whereas the production[4] becomes more real to the extent that finally, out of the sum of these sentiments of decline and

V,284

becoming which are infinitely experienced in one moment, there emerges by way of recollection (due to the necessity of the object in the most finite state) a complete sentiment of existence,[5] the initially dissolved; and after this recollection of the dissolved, individual matter has been united with the infinite sentiment of existence through the recollecting of the dissolution, and after the gap between the aforesaid has been closed, there emerges from this union and adequation of the particular of the past and the infinite of the present the actual new state, the next step that shall follow the past one.

Thus, in its recollection, dissolution fully becomes the secure, relentless, daring act which it actually is because both of its ends stand firmly.

However, this idealistic dissolution is distinct from the real one—also, because once again it moves from the infinite-present to the finite-past—in that 1) at every point of the same there exist dissolution and becoming, 2) that a point in its dissolution and becoming together with every other one and 3) every point in its dissolution and becoming are infinitely interwoven with the absolute sentiment of dissolution and becoming, and that everything infinitely permeates, touches, and approaches each other in pain and joy, discord and peace, movement and rest, form and formlessness, and thus that there operates a heavenly fire rather than an earthly one.

Finally, once again because the idealistic dissolution moves in reverse, from the infinite-present to the finite-past, | the idealistic dissolution differs from the real dissolution in that it can be more continuously determined, that it is neither motivated to scramble together with anxious haste several essential points of dissolution and production into one nor to delve into inessential matter, obstinate to the dreaded dissolution and hence also to production, thus into actually deathly matter, nor to restrict itself, one-sidedly and anxiously to the utmost degree, to one point of dissolution and production, and thus to be committed to actually dead matter, but that instead it moves its precise, straight, free course, being at each point of dissolution and production entirely what it can be at that point but only there, hence being truly individual, naturally not forcing onto this point anything inappropriate, diverting, or in and of itself insignificant; rather it moves freely and fully through the individual

point in all its relations with the other points of dissolution and
production which follow the first two points capable of dissolution
and production, namely, the opposed infinite-new and the finite-
old, the real-total and the ideal-particular.

Finally, the idealistic dissolution differs from the so called
real one (since the latter moves, in reverse, from the infinite to
the finite, after it had moved from the finite to the infinite) in
that, due to the ignorance of its beginning and end point, the
dissolution has to appear inevitably as a real nothing, so that all
existence, hence particular, appears as totality, and a sensuous
idealism, an Epicureanism arises, such as Horace, who apparently
used this perspective only dramatically, has depicted it in his
Prudens futuri temporis exitum,[6] pp.; the idealistic dissolution,
then, finally differs from the so called real one is that the former
appears to be a real nothing while the latter, because it is a
development from the ideal-individual to the infinite-real and
from the infinite-real to the ideal-individual, gains substance and
harmony the more it is thought of as a transition from existence
to existence, just as existence gains spirit the more | it is thought
of as having originated from that transition or tending toward
that transition; thus the dissolution of the ideal-individual appears
not as weakening and death, but as a reviving, as growth, the
dissolution of the infinite-new not as annihilating violence, but
as love, and both together as a (transcendental) creative act
whose essence it is to unite the ideal-individual and the real-
infinite, whose product thus is the real-infinite united with the
ideal-individual, where the infinite-real takes on the appearance
of the individual-real and the latter the appearance of the infinite-
real, and where both unite in a mythic state where, with the
opposition of the infinite-real and the finite-ideal, there also ends
the transition to the extent that the latter gains in rest what the
former ones have gained in life, a state to be confused as little
with the lyric infinite-real as it is to be confused, in its origination
during the transition, with the possible epic representation of
the individual-ideal; for in both cases it unites the spirit of the
one with the tangibility [and] sensuousness of the other. It is
tragic in either case, that is, it unites in either case the infinite-
real with the finite-ideal, and both cases are different only in
degree, for also during the transition, spirit and sign, that is to
say, the material of the transition, are a harmoniously-opposed

,286

one, the former with the latter and vice versa (transcendental with isolated) like animated organisms with an organic soul.

Out of this tragic union of the infinite-new and the finite-old, there develops then a new individual in that the infinite-new individualizes itself in its own appearance by acquiring the appearance of the finite-old.

The new individual now strives to isolate itself and free itself from infinity precisely to the extent that from the second perspective the isolated, individual-old strives to universalize and dissolve itself into the infinite sentiment of existence. *The moment when the period of the individual-new ends is where the infinite-new*

IV,287   *relates to the individual-old as a dissolving and unknown power,* | just as in the previous period the new related to the infinite-old as an unknown power; and these two periods are opposed, that is, the first one as the domination of the individual over the infinite, of the particular over the whole, and the second as the domination of the infinite over the individual, the whole over the particular. The end of this second period and the beginning of the third lies at the moment when the infinite-new as sentiment of existence (as "I") relates to the individual-old (the non "I"),
[. . .]

Following these oppositions, tragic union of the characters, following this [union], reciprocal these opposition of the characters and the reverse. Following these, the tragic union of both.

Remarks on "Oedipus"[1]

It will be good, in order to secure for today's poets a bourgeois existence—taking into account the difference of times and institutions—if we elevate poetry today to the *mechane*[2] of the ancients.

When being compared with those of the Greeks, other works of art, too, lack reliability; at least, they have been judged until today according to the impressions which they made rather than according to their lawful calculation and their other mode of operation through which the beautiful is engendered. Modern poetry, however, lacks especially training and craftmanship, namely, that its mode of operation can be calculated and taught and, once it has been learned, is always capable of being repeated reliably in practice. Among mankind, one has to make sure with every thing that it is Something, i.e., that it is recognizable in the medium (*moyen*) of its appearance, that the way in which it is delimited can be determined and taught. Therefore and for higher reasons, poetry is in need of especially certain and characteristic principles and limits.

Thereto, then, belongs that lawful calculation.

Next, one has to see how the content is distinct from this lawful calculation, through what mode of operation and how, in the infinite yet continuously determined relation, the specific content relates to the general calculation; how the course and that which is to be determined, the living meaning which cannot be calculated, are put in relation with the calculable law.

| The law, the calculation, the way in which a sensuous system, man in his entirety develops as if under the influence of the element, and how representation, sensation and reason appear in different successions yet always according to a certain law, exists in tragedy more as a state of balance than as mere succession.

For indeed, the tragic *transport* is actually empty and the least restrained.

Thereby, in the rhythmic sequence of the representations wherein *transport* presents itself, there becomes necessary *what in poetic meter is called cesura*, the pure word, the counter-rhythmic rupture; namely, in order to meet the onrushing change of representations at its highest point in such a manner that very soon there does not appear the change of representation but the representation itself.

Thereby the sequence of the calculation and the rhythm are divided and, as two halves, refer to one another in such a manner that they appear of equal weight.

Now, if the rhythm of the representation is of such a kind that, in excentric rapidity, the *first ones* are more rended forward by the *following ones*, the cesura or counterrhythmic rupture has to lie from *the beginning* so that the first half is as it were protected against the second one; and, precisely because the second one is originally more rapid and seems to weigh more, the equilibrium will incline from the end toward the beginning due to the counteracting cesura.

If the rhythm of the representations is of such a kind that the *following ones* are more pressured by the *beginning ones*, then the cesura will lie more toward the end; for it is the ending which has to be protected as it were against the beginning, and the balance will consequently incline toward the end, because the first half extends further and the equilibrium occurs later. So much for the calculable law.

Now, the first of the tragic laws indicated here is that of "Oedipus."

V,197 | Antigone follows the second one that is mentioned here.

In both plays the speeches of Tiresias form the cesura.

He enters the course of fate as the custodian of the natural power which, in a tragic manner, removes man from his own life-sphere, the center of his inner life into another world and into the excentric sphere of the dead.

2.

The *intelligibility* of the whole rests primarily on one's [ability to] focus on the scene where Oedipus interprets the saying of the oracle *too infinitely*, and is tempted into *nefas*.

Namely, the saying of the oracle states:[3]

In plain words has Phoebus commanded us, the King,
One shall expurgate the country's disgrace
Nourished by this soil, not nourish the incurable.

[ll. 97 ff.]

That could mean: to carry out, in general, a severe and pure trial, to maintain good civil order. Oedipus, however, right afterwards speaks in priestly fashion.

What is the rite
Of purification? etc. [l.98]

And moves into the particular,

Who is this man whose fate the God pronounces? [l.103]

And thus he leads Kreon's thoughts to the terrible pronouncement:

Our master, O Lord, was Laius
In this country, before you piloted the state. [l.104f.]

Thus the saying of the oracle and the story of Laius' death, not necessarily related to it, are brought together. However, in the sentence immediately following, Oedipus' spirit states in furious presentiment [and] knowing all, the *nefas* quite properly by resentfully interpreting the general injunction in particular terms and applying it to a murderer of Laius, and then taking the sin as infinite.

Who so among you knows the son of Labdacus,
Laius, by whose hand he died,
I command him to inform me of everything, etc.

198 | For that man
I accurse, whoever he be, in this land,
Where I hold sovereignty and throne;
Not shall one welcome him, not greet him,

Not take him to sacrifices and not to offerings.
This I am shown
By the divine oracle, of Pytho, etc. [11. 226 ff.]

Hence, in the subsequent conversation with Tiresias, the won-
derfully furious curiosity, because knowledge—after it has broken
through its barriers—as if intoxicated in its great harmonious
form, which can remain, is spurred by itself to know more than
it can bear or contain.

Hence, in the scene with Creon later on, the suspicion,
because the indomitable thought burdened with sad secrets
becomes insecure, and the loyal and certain spirit suffers in furious
excess which, rejoicing in destruction, merely follows the onrushing time.

Hence, in the middle of the play, in the dialogues with
Jocasta, the sad calmness, the stupor, the pathetic naive error
of the heroic man when he tells Jocasta of the supposed place
of [his] birth, of Polybos whom he fears to kill because he is his
father, and of Merope whom he wants to flee in order not to
marry her who is his mother, according to Teiresias' words, since
he told him that he was the murderer of Laius and that Laius
was his father. For already in the famous dispute between him
and Oedipus, Tiresias says:

The man whom you for long
Have searched, threatening and proclaiming
Laius' murder, he is here; as stranger, after the
Speech, he lives with us, yet soon, as native,
Will he be known as Theban and not
Delight in the accident.
Yet he will be known, living with his children
As brother and as father, and of the woman who
Gave birth to him son and husband both; *in one bed with
The father, and his murderer.* [11. 448 ff.]

V,199 | Hence, at the beginning of the second half, in the scene with
the Corinthian messenger, when he is tempted again by life, the
desperate struggle to find himself, the brutal, almost shameless

strife to gain control of himself, the madly wild seeking for a consciousness.

Jocasta

For upwards does Oedipus bend his courage,
In manifold torture, not like a man
Of sense, arrives he at what will be from what was.

[11. 914 ff.]

Oedipus

My dearest, you, my wife's Jocasta's voice!
Why did you call me forth from the house? [1. 950]

Oedipus

So of sickness died, it seems, the old man! [11.962 f.]

Messenger

Yes, and sufficiently measured against the great Time.

It is easy to discern here how Oedipus' spirit rises with the good message; thus the following speeches can appear as more honorably motivated. Here he, who no longer bears with Heraclean shoulders, casts off the royal cares on behalf of the great weakness, in order to gain control of himself.

Well! who should now, my wife, once again
Interrogate the prophetic hearth or
The birds screaming overhead? which prophesied
That I should kill my father! who,
Having died, slumbers under the earth; yet here
I am, and pure is my spear; if he otherwise
Did not die in the dream through me; then he may
Have died of my hand; at the same time he took
Away with him today's prophesies and now lies
In Hades, no longer of worth. [11. 964 ff.]

/,200 | In the end there dominates in the speeches the insane questioning for a consciousness.

Messenger

Well you show, child, that you do not know your deeds.

Oedipus

How, by the gods, say something, old man! [1007 f.]

Oedipus

What do you say. Did not Polybos seed me?

Messenger

Just as much as one of us.

Oedipus

How this? a father resembling noone?

Messenger

A father only. Polybos not; nor I.

Oedipus

Yet why, then, does he call me child? [1017 ff.]

Messenger

I free you, since your toes are tied.

Oedipus

Tremendous curse I carried from the cradle on.

Messenger

So that you are named accordingly.

Oedipus

That, gods! That, mother, father, speak. [1034 ff.]

Jokasta

By the gods, no! do you care for life,
Then do not search, I myself am suffering enough.

Oedipus

Have courage! if I was of three mothers,
Three times a slave, it would not hurt you. [1060 ff.]

V,201 | Oedipus
Break out what will. My ancestry, though
It may be humble, I will see nevertheless.
Rightfully she is ashamed of my low birth,
For women have highflown pride.
Yet I, considering myself a child of fortune,
Of beneficient fortune, shall not be dishonored.
For this is my mother. First little, then mighty,
The fellowmonths contained me.
And of such breeding, I shall not leave such
That I would not search in full: who I am. [1077 ff.]

It is precisely due to this all-searching, all-interpreting [drive], then, that his spirit finally submits to the raw and primitive language of his servants.

Since such people exist under violent conditions, their language, too, speaks in a more violent order, almost in the manner of furies.

3.

The presentation of the tragic rests primarily on the tremendous—how the god and man mate and how natural force and man's innermost boundlessly unite in wrath—conceiving of itself, [rests] on the boundless union purifying itself through boundless separation. *Tes physeos grammateus en ton kalamon apobrechon eunoun.*[4]

Hence the ever-contending dialogue, hence the chorus as contrast to the former. Hence the all too chaste, all too mechanically and correctly closing concatenation among the different parts, within the dialogue, and between chorus and dialogue and the great parts or scenes that consist of the chorus and dialogue. Everything is speech against speech, one cancelling the other.

Thus, in the chorus scenes of "Oedipus," the lamenting, the peaceful and the religious, the pious lie ("If I am an augur," etc.) and, to the degree of utmost exhaustion, the compassion for a dialogue which will tear apart the soul of just these listeners with its wrathful sensitivity; in the scenes the frightfully festive
V,202   forms, the drama | like an auto-da-fe, as language for a world

where under pest and confusion of senses and under universally inspired prophecy in idle time, with the god and man expressing themselves in the all-forgetting form of infidelity—for divine infidelity is best to retain—so that the course of the world will not show any rupture and the memory of the heavenly ones will not expire.

At such moments man forgets himself and the god and turns around like a traitor, naturally in saintly manner.—In the utmost form of suffering, namely, there exists nothing but the conditions of time and space.

Inside it, man forgets himself because he exists entirely for the moment, the god [forgets himself] because he is nothing but time; and either one is unfaithful, time, because it is reversed categorically at such a moment, no longer fitting beginning and end; man, because at this moment of categorical reversal he has to follow and thus can no longer resemble the beginning in what follows.

Thus Haemon stands in "Antigone." Thus Oedipus himself in the tragedy of "Oedipus."

Remarks on "Antigone"

The rule, the calculable law of "Antigone" compares to that of "Oedipus" like __/____ to _____ so that the balance inclines more from the beginning toward the end than from the end toward the beginning.

It is one of the various successive modes through which representation, sensation and reason develop according to poetic logic. Just as philosophy always treats only one faculty of the soul, such as that the presentation of this one faculty constitutes a whole and that the mere cohering of the parts of this one faculty is called logic, so poetry treats the various faculties of man, such that the depiction of these various faculties constitutes a whole and that the cohering of the more autonomous parts of the various faculties can be called rhythm, in the higher sense, or the calculable law.

If, however, the rhythm of these representations is of such a kind that in the rapidity of enthusiasm the former ones are rent forward by the following ones, then the cesura (a) or the counterrhythmic rupture has to lie from the beginning so that the first half is as it were protected against the second one; and, because the second one is originally more rapid and seems to weigh more, the equilibrium will incline from the end (b) toward the beginning (c) c__ª____b, due to the counteracting cesura.

However, if the rhythm of the representations is such that the succeeding are more pressured by the beginning ones, then the cesura (a) will lie more toward the end; for it is the end which | has to be protected as it were against the beginning, and the equilibrium will consequently incline more toward the end (b) because the first half (c) extends further and the equilibrium occurs later. c____/ª__b

2.

> "What did you dare, to break such law?"
> "Hence, *my* Zeus, he did not report to me
> In this house yet, the right of the death-gods etc."
>
> [11. 449f.]

The boldest moment in a day's course or in a work of art is when the spirit of time and nature, when the heavenly which takes hold of man and the object in which he is interested, oppose one another most ferociously, because the sensuous object extends only half of the way while the spirit awakens most powerfully where the second half sets in. At this moment, man has to *sustain himself the most*; hence, he also is most exposed in his character.

The tragic-moderate weariness of time,[1] whose object is ultimately not of interest to the heart, follows the onrushing spirit of time most intemperately, and the latter appears intemperate then, not in that it spared mankind like a spirit at day, but it is relentless as the spirit of the eternally living, unwritten wasteland and of the world of the dead.

Kreon

Evil ones, though, are not to be considered like good ones.

Antigone

Who is to say; there may be a different custom down there. [1. 520 f.]

The amiable, the understanding in misfortune. The dreaming naive. The true language of Sophocles, since Aeschylus and Euripides know more how to depict suffering and wrath, yet less how to depict man's understanding as wandering below the unthinkable.

Kreon

If I stay faithful with my origins, do I lie?

| Haemon
That you are not, if you do not honor god's name.
                                              [11. 744 f.]

rather than: "if you trod on the god's honor." It was necessary,
it seems, to change the sacred expression here, since it is significant in the middle as seriousness and as autonomous word
wherein everything else finds and transfigures itself.
    Neither the way in which time reverses in the middle nor
how a character categorically follows the categorical time nor
how it proceeds from the Greek to the Hesperian are changeable,
but the sacred name under which the highest is felt or occurs.
The speech refers to the oath of Kreon.

Not long will you
brood under the jealous sun. [1. 1065]

On earth, among mankind, the sun as it becomes physically
relative, can also become truly relative in a moral sense.

I have heard that equal to the desert had become etc.
                                              [11. 824 ff.]

Presumably the noblest trait of Antigone. To the extent
that sacred madness is the highest human manifestation and here
more soul than language, the sublime mockery surpasses all her
other statements and it is also necessary to talk in the superlative
of the beauty, because the attitude is, among other things, also
based on the superlative of human spirit and heroic virtuosity.
    It is a great resource of the secretly working soul that at
the highest state of consciousness it evades consciousness and
that, before the present god actually seizes it, the soul confronts
him with bold, frequently even blasphemic word and thus maintains the sacred living potential of the spirit.
    In a high state of consciousness, then, it always compares
itself to objects that do not have any consciousness, yet which
in their destiny assume the form of consciousness. One such
object is land that has become a desert, which in originally
abundant fertility increases the effects of sunlight too much and

therefore dries out. The fate of the Phrygian Niobe; as everywhere, the destiny of innocent nature which, in its virtuosity,
everywhere moves into the overly organic to the extent | that
man approaches the aorgic[2] under heroic conditions and senti-
ments. And Niobe, then, also represents the image of early
genius.

> She counts to her father the time.
> The striking of the hours, the golden ones. [11. 950f.]

rather than: "administered for Zeus the golden stream of becoming." To bring it closer to our mode of representation. Whether
more or less determined, one apparently has to say Zeus. To be
serious, rather say: "father of time or: father of earth," for it is
his character, opposing the eternal tendency, to reverse *the striving from this world to the other* into a striving *from another world
to this one.* For we have to present the myth everywhere more
conclusively. The golden stream of becoming apparently refers
to the rays of light which also belong to Zeus to the extent that
the time referred to is more calculable through those rays. This,
however, it is whenever time is measured in suffering, for then
the soul follows, feeling much more with the change of time and
thus understanding the plain course of the hours, without the
intellect anticipating the future based on the present.

However, since this firmest staying in the face of changing
time, the heroic hermit-life, the highest state of consciousness
is real, the following chorus is motivated as purest universality
and as the essential point of view where the whole must be
grasped.

For as contrast to the all too inward of this preceding passage, the chorus contains the highest impartiality of the two
opposing personalities who delimit the actions of the other characters in the play.

Once, that which characterizes the Antitheos,[3] where
someone, in the sense of god, acts as if against god and recognizes
the spirit of the highest as lawless. Then, the pious fear of destiny,
thus the praise of god, as something preordained. This is the
spirit of the two impartially contrasted opposites in the chorus.
Antigone acting more in the first sense. Kreon in the second.

V,269 Both insofar as they are contrasted, not like the national and antinational, hence constructed | matter, like Ajax and Ulysses, not like Oedipus against the Greek peasants nor like the original ancient temper as free spirit against loyal simplicity, but equally balanced and different only in time, so that the one mainly loses because it begins, the other wins because it follows. Insofar the strange chorus discussed here fits in most aptly with the whole, and its cold impartiality is warmth precisely because it is so peculiarly apt.

3.

As has been hinted at in the remarks on "Oedipus," the tragic representation has as its premise that the immediate god is all at one with man (for the god of an apostle is more mediate, is highest intellect in highest spirit), that the *infinite* enthusiasm conceives of itself *infinitely*, that is, in consciousness which can-cels consciousness, separating itself in sacred manner, and that the god is present in the figure of death.

Hence, as is already touched on in the remarks on "Oed-ipus," the dialogic form and the chorus in contrast to it, hence the precarious form in the scenes which, following the particu-larly Greek manner, concludes in a necessarily factual manner in the sense that the word turns *more mediately factual* by taking hold of the sensuous body; following our time and mode of rep-resentation, more immediate by taking hold of the more spiritual body. *The Greek-tragic word is deadly-factual,* for the body which it seizes truly kills. For us, existing under the more real Zeus who not only stays between this earth and the ferocious world of the dead, but who also forces the eternally anti-human course of nature on its way to another world *more decidedly down onto earth,* and since this greatly changes the essential and patriotic repre-sentations, and since our poetry must be patriotic so that its themes are selected according to our world-view and their rep-resentations patriotic, for us, then, the Greek representations V,270 change insofar as it is their chief tendency | to comprehend themselves, which was their weakness; on the other hand, it is the main tendency in the mode of representation of our time to designate something, to possess a skill, since the lack of destiny, the *dysmoron*,[4] is our deficiency. Hence, the Greek also possesses more skill and athletic virtue and needs to have these as genuine qualities and serious virtues, however paradoxical the heroes of the *Iliad* may appear to us. For us, these are more subordinated to propriety. And thus the Greek modes of representation and poetic forms are also more subordinated to the patriotic ones.

And hence *the deadly factual, the actual murder with words has to be considered more a specifically Greek artform, subordinate to a more patriotic one.* As can well be demonstrated, a patriotic one may be more murderous-factual than deadly-factual; it ends not in murder and death, for the tragic must be comprehended herein, but more in the manner of *Oedipus at Colonus*, such that the enthusiastic word is terrible and kills, not concretely Greek, in the athletic and plastic spirit where the word seizes the body so that it is the latter which kills.

Thus the tragic presentation, whether more Greek or more Hesperian, is based on a rather violent or irresistable dialogue and chorus which, holding or interpreting the dialogue, as suffering organs of the divinely struggling body lend direction and force to the infinite struggle, organs, which clearly cannot be missing, because in tragic-infinite form, too, the god cannot communicate himself to the body in an absolutely immediate manner but must be conceived as intelligible or appropriate living form; however, the tragic presentation principally consists of the factual word which, being more a relation than something that is stated explicitly, moves by destiny from the beginning to the end; in the specific course of events, in the grouping of characters against one another, and in the mode of reason which is formed in the terrible weariness of tragic time and which later in human time—presenting itself through oppositions, in its wild origin—is considered a firm notion engendered by divine destiny.

V,271 | The course of events in "Antigone" is that of a rebellion where, to the extent that it is a patriotic cause, it is important that everything senses itself as being seized by infinite reversal and, being deeply affected, senses itself in an infinite form within which it is affected. For patriotic reversal is the reversal of all modes and forms of representation. However, an absolute reversal of these, as indeed an absolute reversal altogether without any point of rest is forbidden for man as a knowing being. And in patriotic reversal where the entire form of things changes, and where nature and necessity, which always remain, incline toward another form—be it that they transcend into chaos or into a new form—in such a change everything that is merely necessary favors the change; hence, given the possibility of such a change, the neutral [one] too, (and not only he who is directed against the patriotic form by a spiritual force of the time), can be forced to be patriotic, to be present in infinite form, the religious, political and moral form of his fatherland (*prophanethi theos*).[5] Such serious remarks are also necessary for the understanding of the Greek as well as of all true works of art. The actual mode of procedure in a rebellion, then (which, of course, is only one form of patriotic reversal, and which has still a more determined character), has just been hinted at.

If such a phenomenon is tragic, it moves by way of reaction, and the informal is kindled by the all-too-formal. Hence, what is characteristic here is that the individuals enclosed by *such* a destiny do not appear, like in "Oedipus," as a manifestation of ideas, as disputing the truth, not as something resisting understanding, and also not as something defending life, property or honor, like the characters in "Ajax," but that they confront one another as individuals in the stricter sense, as persons of rank, that they become formalized.

The grouping of such individuals can be compared, as in "Antigone," to a competition of runners where the first one to breathe heavily and to jostle the opponent has lost, since one can compare the struggling in "Oedipus" to a fistfight, that in "Ajax" to a match of fencing.

V,272 | The form of reason which takes shape here as a tragic one is political, namely republican, since the equilibrium between Kreon and Antigone, between the formal and counter-formal, is kept too equal. This is particularly evident toward the end where Kreon is almost abused by his servants.

Sophocles is right. It is this the destiny of his age and the form of his fatherland. One may indeed idealize, e.g., choose the most opportune moment, yet the patriotic modes of representation, at least as regards the subordination, must not be changed by the poet who depicts the world on a reduced scale.

For us such a form is relevant precisely because the infinite, like the spirit of the states and of the world, cannot be grasped other than from an askew perspective. The patriotic forms of our poets, where there are such, are still to be preferred, for such do not merely exist in order to comprehend the spirit of the age but in order to grasp and feel it once it has been understood and learned.

SELECTED LETTERS

No. 41   To his Mother[1]

Dearest Mother!

You have altogether ashamed me with your benevolence. I am still so far behind you as regards goodness, and you give me so much opportunity to imitate you. Please forgive me, dearest mother!, if in my last letter I dropped a word that may be in conflict with a child's respect.—I am fully serious about the rejection of the travel to Nürtingen. During the short time of my stay I could be with you only very little, and I cannot obtain permission for a longer stay. Yet if it is possible, I shall still come during this month.—Here you have my prayer from yesterday (that is, Sunday). This time, I was somewhat more far-reaching than in my first one. I elaborated on a matter whose understanding becomes dearer to me with every day. For a longer time than usual, I have been occupying myself with that part of the prayer wherein it is said that *without belief in Christianity* there would occur *no religion whatsoever, no certainty of God and immortality.* I believe that there are many good Christians who are not convinced by that statement in its entire scope; not that they do not believe when the statement is developed, but because they never confront the situations where they get to know the entire necessity of the Christian religion. Allow me, dear mother!, to tell you how I was gradually led to that point. I studied that part of world-wisdom which deals with *proofs of reason* for the existence of god and with his characteristics, which we are to learn from nature, with an interest of which I am not ashamed, even though for some time it led me to thoughts that might have alarmed you, had you known them. Namely, I suspected that those *proofs of reason* for the existence of God and also for immortality were so imperfect | that they could be overthrown entirely or at least in their main parts by accute opponents. During this

119

time I got into my hands writings about and by Spinoza, a great [and] honorable man from the last century and yet, strictly speaking, an atheist. I found that, if one examines them carefully [and] with reason, with the cold reason abandoned by the heart, one must arrive at his ideas, namely, if one wants to explain everything. Yet at that point, there was left for me the belief of my heart which so unambiguously yearns for the eternal, for god. However, do we not doubt that the most which we wish (as I say in my prayer as well)? Who helps us out of these labyrinths?— Christ. He shows by way of miracles that he is what he says of himself, that he is God. He teaches us the existence of the deity, the love and wisdom and all-mightiness of the deity so clearly. And he must know that a God and what God is, for he is most intimately connected with the divinity. [It] is God himself.

For one year that has been the course of my insights regarding the deity.

A thousand greetings to my dear Rike, and to Karl who please shall send me something.—I shall be happy, if the dear *Oncle* becomes priest in Lochgau. Perhaps this is the place where I will be able some day to live quiet vicar's years.—For what you have sent I express thousand thanks

I am

Your
most obedient son
Fritz

No. 60   To Neuffer[1]

You are right, my heart's brother! Your genius was very close to me these days. Indeed, I felt the eternal of your love to me rarely with such certainty and silent joy. For some time, your genius has conveyed to me even your Being, as I believe. I wrote to our Stäudlin[2] of many blessed hours which I now spend. You See! it was because your soul lived within me. I felt your calmness, your beautiful contentment with which you look onto the present and the future, onto nature and mankind. Also your bold | hopes with which you look onto our great goal live in me. To be sure, I wrote to Stäudlin: Neuffer's quiet flame will shine increasingly brighter when, perhaps, my straw-fire will have evaporated long ago; yet this just does not always frighten me, the least during those divine hours when I return from the womb of inspiring nature or from the grove at Ilissus where, resting among disciples of Plato, I would follow with my eyes the flight of the magnificent one as he roves through the dark distances of the primal world, or where, with dizziness, I would follow him into the utmost depth, to the remotest regions of the land of spirit, where the soul of the world emanates its life into the thousand pulses of nature, whereto the effluvious forces return in their immesurable circle, or when, intoxicated by the Socratic chalice and by Socratic friendship, I would listen at the meal to the enchanted youths as they would pay tribute to the sacred love with tender, fiery speech, and how the jester Aristophanes would poke fun underneath, and finally how the master, the divine Socrates himself with his heavenly wisdom would teach them all what is love—there,[3] friend of my heart, I am of course not so despondent and think sometimes that I ought to be able to communicate a sparkle of the tender flame that warms and illuminates me at such moments to my little work in which I truly live and weave, my *Hyperion*,[4] and also bring forth something for the delight of the people.

I soon found that my hymns will rarely win sympathy among those whose hearts are more beautiful, and this supported me in my conception of a Greek novel. Let your noble female friends judge, based on the fragment that I sent to our Stäudlin today, whether my *Hyperion* might not some day fill a little space among the heroes who indeed entertain us somewhat better than the knights rich in words and adventures. Especially, I am eager to hear the judgment of that person of whom you make no mention. I hope that what follows shall reconcile her and others with a harsh passage about her gender which had to be spoken out of

VI,87   the soul of Hyperion. Judge for yourself, | too, dear brother! The perspective from which I would like this fragment to be looked at, I have elaborated with tedious length in the letter to Stäudlin. I wish I was able to write you what is most essential about it this time. Yet time probably will not suffice. Only so much. This fragment seems more a mixture of random moods than the reflected development of a tightly grasped character, because I still leave undetermined the motives for the ideas and sensations and do so because I wanted to occupy more the faculty of taste with a painting of ideas and sensations (for aesthetic gratification) than reason with balanced psychological development. Of course, in the end everything must be traceable back to the character and to the circumstances that affect it. Whether this is the case with my novel, the future will show.

Perhaps I have chosen exactly the least interesting fragment. Furthermore, the necessary prior conditions, without which the following can be enjoyed even less, that is, the entire second book without the first, still unfinished one, these necessary prior conditions had to be there as well.—What you have said so beautifully about the *terra incognita* in the realm of poetry, pertains especially to a novel. Enough predecessors, few that discovered new and beautiful territory, and still immeasurable realms to be discovered and worked with! This I promise you solemnly, that if the whole of my *Hyperion* will not be three times better than this fragment, it will be thrust into fire without mercy. In general, if posterity will not be my judge, if I cannot say that soon and with certainty to myself, then I will tear, like you, every string from my lyre and bury it in the waste of time. Your song has pleased me very, very well, especially this last stanza.

Is it not true, dear brother! This last stanza belongs to those where one unmasks the veiled deities of philosophy? What I envy you most for is, as I believe I have already told you many times, your radiant presentation. I struggle for it with all might. Yet the dear guest, your song would have attained an even friendlier countenance, | if it had joined the company of your hymn. I almost believe you would do with this hymn as some jester may have done in the tournament. He would not appear until the enemy entered the arena rather confidently and then humiliated the poor chap with his unexpected victory all the more. Come, come! I am ready for anything. I sent my hymn[5] to our Stäudlin. The magic light in which I saw it once I was done with it, and even more once I had communicated it to you on that unforgettable afternoon, has vanished by now so entirely that I can only console myself about its shortcomings by hoping for a better hymn to come soon.—Incidentally, what is the situation of the journal?—Have you already written to Matthison?[6]—I haven't yet. Here, my [copy of] Hesiod.

VI,88

Ah! you are of course right in that it should be a delightful, productive time if we could live together again, as before. I will try all I can to see you soon. And now, farewell!

Your
Hölderlin

The parcel to Stäudlin was already packed when, this morning, your dear letter arrived. May I ask you to bring it to him?

No. 94   To Hegel

Jena, January 26, '95

Your letter was a happy welcome to my second arrival at Jena. I had departed around the end of December with Major von Kalb's wife,[1] and with my disciple with whom I had spent here two months, for Weimar without suspecting so soon a return. The manifold miseries which I had to experience because of the specific circumstances that occurred with my subject [student], in the educational field, my fragile health, and the need to live at least some time for myself which was only increased by my stay here, caused me even before my departure for Jena to tell the Major's wife about my wish to leave the position. I let myself be persuaded by her and Schiller to make one more attempt, yet could not bear it longer than 14 days, because it also cost me, among other things, almost my entire nightly rest, and I returned now in full peace to Jena into an independence which I basically enjoy for the first time in my life and which hopefully will not be unproductive. My productive activity is by now almost entirely directed onto the reforming of the materials from my novel. The fragment in *Thalia* is one of these raw masses. I think that I will finish with it until Easter; let me keep silence about it in the meantime. The "Genius der Kühnheit" which you perhaps still

remember, I have revised [and] submitted, | together with some other poems, to *Thalia.* Schiller shows much care for me and has encouraged me to submit contributions for his new journal, *Die Horen,*[2] and also for his new muses' almanac.

With Goethe I have spoken, [my] brother! It is the most beautiful pleasure in our lives to find so much humanity together with so much greatness. He conversed with me so gently and politely that, quite truly, my heart rejoiced and still does when I think of it. Herder also was very polite, took my hand, yet displayed more the man of the world; he often spoke as much in allegorical manner as you know him too; presumably I will again visit them sometime; the Major von Kalb's family will most likely stay on in Weimar (for which reason the boy also was no longer in need of me and my leave could be accelerated), and the friendship which I have especially with the Major's wife, allows me frequent visits at this house.

Fichte's speculative writings—*Foundation of the Entire Science of Knowledge*—also his published lectures about the *Destination of the Scholar* will interest you very much.[3] In the beginning, I suspected him very much of dogmatism; he appears, if I may speculate, to have stood very much at the crossroads, or still to stand there—he wants to move in theory beyond the fact of consciousness; many of his statements show that, and that is just as certain and even more strikingly transcendent than if the metaphysicians so far would move beyond the existence of the world—his absolute "I" (= Spinoza's Substance) contains all reality; it is everything, and outside of it there is nothing; hence there is no object for this "I," for otherwise not all reality would be within it; however, a consciousness without object cannot be thought, and if I myself am this object, then I am as such necessarily restricted, even if it were only within time, hence not absolute; therefore, within the absolute "I," no consciousness is conceivable; as absolute "I" I have no consciousness, and insofar as I have no consciousness I am (for myself) nothing, hence is the absolute "I" (for me) nothing.[4]

VI,156
Thus I took down my thoughts in Waltershausen when I read his first pages, | immediately after the reading of Spinoza; Fichte confirmed [. . .][5] His dealings with the reciprocal determination of the "I" and the "Non-I" (following his language) is certainly strange, also the idea of striving and more.[6] I have to break off and ask you to consider all this as not written. That you are approaching the concept of religion is surely in various respects good and important.[7] The concept of predestination you will probably treat entirely in parallel with Kant's teleology; the way in which he combines the mechanism of nature (hence also of destiny) with its purposefulness seems to me to contain indeed the entire spirit of his system; it is certainly the same purposefulness by means of which he reconciles all antinomies. With respect to the antinomies, Fichte has a very strange notion about

which I will rather write you another time. I have been dealing for a long time with the ideal of a public education, and because you concern yourself right now with a part of it, religion, I perhaps chose your image and your friendship as the *conductor* of the thoughts into the outer, sensuous world and write to you what I probably would have written later, at an adequate time, in letters that you shall judge and correct.

No. 97   *To his Brother*

Jena, April 13, 1795

I have been your debtor for a long time, dear brother. But the joy that you gave me with the manifold expressions of your brotherly, pure heart cannot be compensated with words in any case. In fact, I don't know how I shall deserve so much love which I experience from all my dear ones.

The goodness of our dear mother shames me infinitely. Even if she were not our mother, and if this goodness was not bestowed upon me, I would have to be eternally happy that such a soul exists on earth. O, my Karl! How much our duty is alleviated for us! No human heart could be within us, if the sympathy of such a mother did not strengthen us infinitely in our spiritual maturation.—I believe that you are on the right way, dear brother! In your heart there exists the unselfish sense of duty; your spirit develops for itself this sense with the help of other noble spirits whose writings prove your friends; the feeling of your heart becomes a purely thought [and] incorruptible principle; thought does not kill it; it is secured, fastened by thought. On that idea of duty, that is, on the principle: man should always act in such a manner that the attitude out of which he acts could function as the law for everyone;[1] and he shall act simply because he shall, because it is the sacred, unchangeable law of his being (as everybody can find who with an impartial eye examines his conscience, the feeling of that law which manifests itself in individual acts),— on that sacred law of our morality, then, you found the judgments of your rights; to increasingly approximate that sacred law is your ultimate purpose, the goal of all your striving and this goal you share with everything that is called man; now, what remains necessary as the means to that highest goal, everything which is indispensable for the never accomplished perfection of your morality to which you are entitled, what is most indispensable

VI,163   here is | certainly the freedom of will (how could we do good, if we could not will the good? what happens due to coercion is not the act of a good will, hence not good in the actual sense, perhaps useful, yet not good, perhaps legal, yet not moral); and thus none of your forces can be restricted in a manner that would render it more or less useless for your destination and [would be] no product of your forces; whenever you do not allow for such a restriction of your forces or of its products, you claim a right, be it with words or deeds. Of course, every man also has equal rights in this sense; noone, whoever he be, can be denied the use of his forces or their products in any way that would more or less prevent him from coming closer to his goal, the highest-possible morality.—

However, because this goal is impossible on earth, because it cannot be attained at any time, for we can only approach it in an infinite progress, the belief in an infinite continuity is necessary, since the infinite progress in the good is an incontrovertible postulate of our law; this infinite continuity however, is not conceivable without a belief in a lord of nature whose will wills the same which the law of morality is asking within us, who therefore must will our infinite continuity because he wills our infinite progress in the good, and who, as the lord of nature, also has the might to realize what he wills. Naturally, this is to speak of him in human terms, for the will and the deed of the infinite are one. And thus there is founded on the sacred law inside us the reasonable belief in God and immortality, also in the wise guidance of our destinies insofar as they do not depend on us; for as certain as the highest purpose is highest morality, as necessary as it is for us to take this purpose as the highest one, so necessary is the belief for us that where our will's might does not suffice—they may go as they will—things nevertheless work together for that purpose, that is, are arranged by a sacred, wise

VI,164   being that has the might where | ours does not suffice. I see that I ought to say a good deal more, yet I break off, because I wish to tell you, as well as can be done with few words, about a main peculiarity of the Fichtean philosophy.[2] "There is within man a striving into the infinite, an activity which indeed does not allow him any barrier as everlasting, indeed no stagnation, but strives to become increasingly widespread, free, independent; this in its drive infinite activity is restricted; the unrestricted activity, infinite in its drive, is necessary in the nature of a conscious being (of an "I," as Fichte calls it), yet the restriction of this activity, too, is necessary for a conscious being, for if the activity were not restricted, not imperfect, this activity would be everything, and nothing would exist outside of it; if, then, our activity did not suffer any resistance from the outside, nothing would exist outside us, we would not know of anything, we would have no consciousness; if nothing was opposed to us, there would be no object; yet as necessary as the restriction, the resistance and the suffering effected by resistance are for consciousness, so necessary is the striving for the infinite, an activity, infinite in its drive, within the being which has consciousness; for if we did not strive to be infinite, free of all barriers, we would not feel either that something was opposed to this striving, hence we once again would not feel anything different from ourselves, we would not know anything, we would not have a consciousness."—I have made myself as clear as possible given the brevity with which I had to express myself. At the beginning of this winter, until I had worked my way into it, this matter caused me occasionally headaches, all the more since from my study of Kantian philosophy I was used to verify before accepting.—Niethammer has also asked me to join work at his "Philosophical Journal,"[3] and thus I have quite a bit of work ahead for this summer. Following Schiller's initiative,[4] Cotta has taken into commission my little work about which I already wrote; | how much he will pay me shall be arranged—so Schiller wants it—when Cotta comes here, which will be the case in about fourteen days. I hope not to be a burden any longer to our dear mother. I thank you for what you mailed with all my heart's gratitude; I will never forget that in my present situation I was supported with such benevolence.

Schiller will presumably stay on. If I stay here, I will probably take my exams next autumn. This is the only condition that allows me to hold lectures. The title of a professor is of no importance to me, and a professor's salary is fair only for a few. Many have none at all.—I still have to tell [you] something about a little pleasure trip which I undertook, because my urge for movement was very strong after the constant sitting throughout the winter, and because I had some spare money. Yet I keep

I,165

it for a letter to my dear Rike.—The beautiful promised vest I will accept with much gratitude. However, perhaps the dear mother will not consider it ungrateful if I confess that I have yet unworked vest-material in my suitcase—a gift that I took with me from Waltershausen—yet that I urgently need some pants. It is true, my dear! am I not somewhat indiscreet? I must write to dear Rike next Wednesday, there will not be enough time today.

Farewell, and thousand warm greetings to all.

No. 117 To Immanuel Niethammer[1]

Frankfurt/Main, February 24, 1796.

My honorable friend!

I deferred it from one day to the next to give you notice about me. I probably would be waiting longer with the letter that I owe you, if I was not reminded by you of my promise. You do this so gently that I am extremely ashamed. You ask me how I feel in my new situation and whether I will finish soon with the essays which to write I had promised you back in Jena.

The new circumstances in which I live now are the best ones imaginable. I have much leisure for my own work, and philosophy is once again my almost exclusive occupation. I have taken Kant and Reinhold[2] and hope to collect and strengthen my spirit in this element which was dispelled and weakened by fruitless efforts of which you were a witness.

However, the echoes of Jena still ring too mightily inside me, and the recollection has still too much power as for the present to become healing for me. Various lines intertwine in my mind, and I am unable to unravel them. For | continuous, hard working as the posed philosophical task demands it, I am not yet sufficiently collected.

I am missing your company. You are still my philosophical mentor, and your advice that I should beware of abstract expressions is to me as dear today as it was earlier when I let myself become entangled in it, when I became discordant with myself. Philosophy is a tyrant, and I endure its force more than that I subject myself to it by free choice.

In the philosophical letters, I want to discover the principle which explains to me the divisions in which we think and exist,

131

yet which is also capable of dispelling the conflict between subject and object, between our self and the world, yes, also between reason and revelation,—theoretically, in intellectual intuition, without our practical reason having to come to our aid.[3] For this we need an aesthetic sense, and I will call my philosophical letters "New Letters on the Aesthetic Education of Man."[4] Also, I will move in [these letters] from philosophy to poetry and religion.

Schelling, whom I saw before my departure, is happy to participate in your journal and to be introduced by you to the learned world.[5] We did not always speak in agreement, yet we agreed that new ideas can be presented most appropriately in letter-form. As you will know, he has shifted to a new road with his new convictions before he would have reached the goal on the worse one. Tell me what you think about his latest ideas.

Give my regards to everyone who holds me in kind remembrance, and maintain for me your friendship which was so dear to me. It would be the most beautiful reward for me, if I could please you with fruits of which I could say that their ripening was advanced by your care and attention.

Your
Hölderlin.

No. 121   To his Brother

Frankfurt, June 2, 1796

Dear Brother!

Your last letter has given me infinite joy. Goethe says somewhere: "Lust and Love are the wings for great deeds."—Such is also the case with truth; he who loves it will find it; he whose heart elevates itself most above the anxious, egoistic spectrum in which most people grow up and which we, unfortunately! find almost everywhere on the part of the "earth" which we are assigned for rest and work, [he] whose soul is not conceited, his spirit will not be properly conceited either.

Your striving and struggling renders your spirit increasingly strong and flexible, dear Karl! You seem to go deeper and to look into more than one direction.

This, then, is also true profundity, namely: complete knowledge of the parts that we must found and combine into one, and deep knowledge of that which founds and comprehends, piercing to the farthest end of knowledge. Reason, one can say, lays the foundation with its principles, the laws of acting and thinking, to the extent that they are merely referred to the universal contradiction within man, namely, to the contradiction between the striving for the absolute and the striving for restriction. However, those principles of reason are themselves founded by reason in that it refers them to the Ideal, to the highest foundation of all; and the "must" which is implicit in all principles of reason is in this manner dependent on (idealistic) Being. Now, if the principles of reason which order that the contradiction of that universal, self-opposed striving be united (according to the ideal of beauty), if these principles are universally enacted in that contradiction, then any resolution of the | conflict must have a result, and these results of the universal resolution of the conflict are then the general concepts of understanding, e.g., the concepts of substance and accident, of action and reaction, duty and right, etc. These concepts are to understanding only what the ideal is to reason; as reason forms its laws following the ideal, so understanding forms its maxims following these concepts. These maxims contain the criteria and conditions under which any activity or object must be subjected to those general concepts. For instance, I have the right to appropriate a matter that does not exist under the disposition of a free will. General concept: right. Condition: it exists not under the disposition of a free will. The activity subjected to the general concept: appropriation of a matter.

I write you this in the manner in which one encloses a hasty drawing or something else in a letter for the purpose of a brief conversation.

That your fate weighs heavily on you I believe you readily, my dear! Be a man and win. The slavery which invades our heart and spirit from all sides, in early youth and mature age, the mistreatment and suffocation of our noblest strengths also gives us the great sense of self when we carry out our better purposes. I will also do my part. I cannot and will not procure you another position. You simply need leisure now; you must be able to live with yourself before you live for others. Out of regard for you I propose to you, contrary to what I have said otherwise, that you visit a university. If my fickle destiny keeps me in my present situation, I will be able to spare 200 fl. around the end of next winter; I will send them to you, and you will go to Jena and can count, I believe, every year on the same sum from me, and the little more that you may still be in need of, our dear mother won't deny you.| Do not thank me, my conviction asks this of me, and the fulfilment of a duty does not allow for another compensation than that we reach our goal. And how could we doubt that, dear brother!

VI,210

Of important acquaintances, in the sense that you mean it, I can write you unfortunately very little or nothing.

Let the world run its course if it cannot be halted; we will go our way.

I hope to work more this summer than before. The drive to create something out of ourselves, which will remain when we part, actually is what alone ties us to life.

To be sure, we also frequently long to transcend from this intermediary state of life and death into the infinite being of the beautiful world, into the arms of eternally youthful nature from where we emerged. Yet everything goes its steady course; why should we hurry prematurely whereto we all strive.

The sun shall not put us to shame after all. It rises above evil and good; thus we can remain for a while among men and their activities and under our own barrier and weakness.—If possible, I will take care of your friend H. Sinclair,[1] whom I visited only recently, has me send you his regards. He mourns as we do.

Fichte has published a natural law; At this moment, I am receiving it from the bookseller [and] cannot judge it yet. Still, I think I can advise you with good reason to buy it.

Thousand greetings to our dear mother and other relatives and friends!

Farewell, my Karl!

Your
Hölderlin.

Cotta unfortunately detains me. Hopefully he will have sent the money or sends it soon, even though the print of my book starts only now.

No. 172   To his Brother

[. . .]¹

VI,302   Right now the clock rings twelve and the year '99 begins. A fortunate year for you, my dearest, and for all our family! And then a great, happy century for Germany and the world!

So I will lie down to sleep.

Jan. 1, 1799

Today, I had put aside my usual occupations and in my idleness had various thoughts concerning the interest that the Germans take in speculative philosophy, then again in political literature, and then also, however to a lesser degree, in poetry. Perhaps you have read a small amusing essay in the "*Allgemeine Zeitung*" about the German poets.² This was what led me into it for the first time, and since you and I rarely practice philosophy VI,303 now, | you will not find it useless if I write down for you these thoughts of mine.

The fortunate influence which the philosophical and political readings have on the education of our nation is incontrovertible, and perhaps the national character of the Germans, if I have inferred rightly from my very incomplete experience, was for a while more in need of that dual influence than of any other. For I believe that the most common virtues and shortcomings of the Germans boil down to a rather conceited domesticity. They are everywhere *glebae addicti*,³ and the majority is in some manner, literally or metaphorically, tied to its soil; and if it went on like this they would eventually have to drag to their death the burden of their lovely (moral and physical) acquisitions and inheritances, just like that good-hearted Dutch painter. Everyone is only at home where he has been born and can and will hardly move beyond that with his interests and concepts. Hence that lack of flexibility, of drive, of manifold development of strengths, hence the sinister, abjecting timidity or also the fearful, submissive and blind devotion with which they accept everything that lies outside their anxious, narrow sphere; hence, too, this insensitivity to communal honor and communal property which, of course, generally exists among the modern people yet to an eminent degree with the Germans. And just as only he is happy in his chamber who also lives in the open field, so the individual life that is proper to everyone cannot exist without universality and an open outlook on the world; and indeed, among the Germans the one has perished with the other as it seems, and it is not to the credit of the apostles of limitedness that among the ancients, where everyone belonged to the surrounding world with sense and soul, there is to be found much more inwardness in individual characters and situations than, for example, among us Germans; and the conceited outcry against coldhearted cosmopolitanism and exaggerated metaphysics cannot be disproven more truthfully than by a noble pair like Thales | and Solon who travelled together through Greece and Egypt and Asia in order to become acquainted with the constitutions and philosophers of the world;[4] who therefore were universalized in more than one respect, yet who were quite good friends and more humane and even more naive than all those taken together who would like to persuade us that, in order to preserve our naturalness, we should not open to the world—which is always worth it—our eyes and hearts.

1,304

Now, since the Germans mostly existed in this anxiously conceited state, they could not experience a more beneficial influence than that of the new philosophy which insists to the extreme on the universality of cognitive interest and which uncovers the infinite striving within man; and even if it keeps too one-sidedly to the great autonomy of human nature, it still is, as the philosophy of the epoch, the only possible one.

Kant is the Moses of our nation who leads it out of the Egyptian apathy into the free, solitary desert of his speculation and who brings the rigorous law from the sacred mountain. Of course, they still dance around their golden cows and hunger for their meats, and he actually would have to emigrate with them into some recluse if they were to abstain from the dead customs and opinions that have become heart- and spiritless and under which their better, more living nature moans like in deep dungeon.

From the other side, political literature must take a likewise positive effect, especially if the phenomena of our era are presented in a forceful and competent manner. The horizon of man enlarges, and with the daily outlook on the world there also originates and increases the interest in the world, and the sense of universality and the elevation above the personal, narrow sphere of life is certainly advanced through the notion of the widespread human society and its great destinies as through the philosophical commandment to universalize the interest and the perspective; and like the warrior who, when collaborating with the army, feels more | courageous and mighty, and who indeed is so, thus man's strength and agility grows to the extent that the sphere of his life enlarges wherein he feels that he participates and empathizes (if, on the other hand, the sphere does not expand so far that the individual is lost too much within the whole). Incidentally, the interest for philosophy and politics, even if it were more universal and serious than it is, remains nothing less than sufficient for the education of our nation, and it would be desirable that some day the infinite misunderstanding would come to an end by which art and particularly poetry are degraded for those who engage in them and who want to enjoy them. Much has already been said about the influence of the arts on the education of mankind, yet it was always expressed as though nobody was serious about it, and that was natural, for they did not consider what art, and particularly poetry, are in their essence. They only referred to its unassuming exterior appearance, which of course is separable from its essence, yet which forms nothing less than the character of art; one took it as play because it appears in the unassuming figure of the play, and hence it logically could not produce a different effect than that of the play, namely distraction, almost the opposite of what it effects where it is present in its true nature. For then man collects himself with it, it affords him a repose, not the empty, but the living repose where all forces are active and are not recognized as active ones only because of their intimate harmony. It nourishes people, and unites them not like the play where they are united only insofar as everyone forgets himself and noone's peculiarity appears.

VI,305

You will forgive, dearest brother! That I am so ponderous
and fragmentary in my letter. Perhaps only few people will have
as much difficulty with the transition from one mood to another
as I do; in particular, I cannot easily find my way out of reasoning
and into poetry, and vice versa. Also, I have been affected these
days by a letter from our dear mother in which she expressed her
happiness about my | religiosity and, among other things, asked
me to write a poem for the birthday of our dear seventy-two year
old grandmother; and several other things in the extremely
touching letter have moved me so much that I spent the time
during which I perhaps would have written you mostly with
thoughts of her and all my dear ones. Indeed, the same evening
that I received the letter, I started a poem for the dear grandmother and almost finished it that night. I thought that it should
make the good mothers happy if I sent off a letter and the poem
the following day. However, the tones which I touched there
resounded so mightily within me, the transformations of my soul
and spirit which I experienced since my youth, past and present
of my life became so sensible to me that later I could not find
any sleep and had trouble to concentrate the following day. That
is how I am. You will wonder, when seeing the poetically so
insignificant verses, how I could have felt so strangely. Yet I
have said very little about what I felt on that occasion. In fact,
I sometimes experience that I convey my most vivid soul in very
flat words, so that no other person than myself knows what I
actually wanted to say.

I will see now whether I can express something of what I
recently wanted to tell you about poetry. I said that poetry unites
man not like the play; it unites people if it is authentic and works
authentically with all the manifold suffring, fortune, striving,
hoping, and fearing, with all their opinions and mistakes, all
their virtues and ideas, with everything major and minor that
exists among them, unites them into a living, a thousand times
divided, inward whole, for precisely this shall be poetry itself;
and like the cause, so the effect. Is it not true, my dear, the
Germans could well use such a *panacea*, even after the politico-
philosophical cure; for, regardless of everything else, the
philosophico-political education already contains in itself the

1,306

inconvenience that it knits together the people in the essential, | inevitably necessary relations, in duty and law; yet how much is left, then, for human harmony? The fore-, middle- and background, drawn according to optic laws, is far from being the landscape which, at most, would like to place itself at the side of nature's live creation. Yet the best among the Germans still think that if the world was only neatly symmetrical everything would be done with. Oh Greece, with your geniality and your piety, whereto have you come? I myself, too, despite all good will, merely stumble in my deeds and thoughts after these only human beings in the world, and in what I do and say I am often only the more inept and inconsistent because I stand, like geese, with my flat feet in the modern water and helplessly beat my wings up to the Greek sky. Do not scold me for the simile. It is unseemly but true, and among ourselves something like that is still acceptable; also it shall only be said of me.

For your encouraging remarks about my little poems and several other friendly and strengthening words in your letter, I thank you a thousand times. We must stay firmly together in all our need and in our spirit. Before everything else, we will accept with all love and seriousness the great word, the *homo sum, nihil humani a me alienum puto*; it shall not render us insincere but only truthful against ourselves, and clairvoyant and tolerant against the world; yet then again we do not want to let ourselves be impeded by any gossip of affectation, exaggeration, ambition, idiosyncracy, etc., in order to struggle with all might and to see with all clearity and tenderness how we arrange everything human within ourselves and others in an increasingly free and intimate relation, be it in visual presentation or in the authentic world; and if the forces of darkness will invade with violent means, we cast the quill under the table and go in God's name where the need is the greatest and where we are most needed. Farewell!

Your
Fritz.

No. 183   To Neuffer

Homburg Heights, July 3, '99

I have not entirely kept my word, my friend! And you receive what was promised a week later than I thought.[1] I was obliged to leave for some days where I also spoke our courageous Jung who right now is doing particularly well.[2] He will give me his Ossian for the Journal. Some pieces may serve me excellently as text for a commentary.

If it should interest you, I will on occasion tell you something about the method and manner in which I wrote "Emilie." You may well imagine that, given the haste with which I had to go to work, I could not express the poetic form, which I had already projected for a rather long time, as I wished and as it would have been necessary in order to render sensible the advantages which it probably has, in particular for themes that are not truly heroic. I am not at all concerned with the appearance of what is new; however, I feel and see more and more how we waver between two extremes, [that] of lawlessness—and the blind subjection under old forms and the attaching constriction and misapplication. Therefore, do not believe, dear friend ! that I arbitrarily give and puzzle out for myself a personal form; I examine my feeling which leads me to this or that and certainly ask myself whether a form which I choose does not contradict the ideal and especially also the subject which it treats. Certainly I can be right in a general sense but get on the wrong track all

the more easily in the execution | because I follow only myself and cannot adhere to any sensuous pattern. Yet there is no other choice; in the way that we treat any subject which is only slightly modern, we must also abandon, as I see it, the old classical forms which are so intimately fitted to their theme that they do not fit any other one. Now, we are certainly used to the fact that, e.g., a love-story, *which is nothing but that*, is presented in the form of a tragedy which, as regards its internal course and its heroic dialogue, for the ancients does not at all suit an actual love-story. If one retains the heroic dialogue, then it always seems as though the lovers were fighting. If one abandons it, then the tone contradicts the actual form of tragedy which then, of course, is also no longer strictly maintained yet which therefore has also lost its peculiar poetic value and significance for us. However, one also wants moving and deeply affecting passages and situations; author and audience hardly ever pay attention to the significance and impression of the whole. And thus the strictest of all poetic forms, which *is entirely designed to advance in harmonious alternation, without any ornament, almost in grand tones of which each one is a proper whole* and which, in this proud denial of anything accidental, depicts the ideal of a living whole as brief and, simultaneously, as completely and full of content as possible, therefore more precise yet also more serious than all other known poetic forms—this honorable tragic form has been degraded to a means in order to occasionally say something shining or tender. Yet, what use could one make of it if one did not choose the fitting subject, combined with which it could alone preserve meaning and life. It had become dead like all other forms when they lost the living soul whom they served like an organic structure out of which they originally developed, as for instance the republican form in our *Reichsstädte* has become dead and meaningless because the people are not of such a kind that they would be *in need* of it, to say the least.

VI,340 | Now, as the tragic themes are made in order to advance in numerous great, autonomous tones with harmonious alternation and to present a whole [which is] full of strong, significant parts with the greatest possible exclusion of anything accidental, so the sentimental themes, e.g., love, are altogether apt to progress with harmonious alternation, even though not with great and proud, firm tones and with decisive denial of anything accidental but with *this gentle shyness of the accidental* and in profound, full, elegaic-significant tones, multi-significant by virtue of the nostalgia and hope which they express, and [they are apt] to present the ideal of a living whole, to be sure, not with this strained force of the parts and this onrushing progression, with this quick brevity, yet with wings, like Psyche and Amor, and with intimate brevity; and now we only ask in what form this can be achieved most naturally and intrinsically, so that the beautiful spirit of love has its own poetic form and mode.

Forgive me, if I cause you boredom with this unspecific reasoning. I live so much alone with myself that I now, in an idle hour, frequently want to converse in writing with an impartial friend about matters that are dear to me and, as you see, render me more talkative than is perhaps pleasant for the other one. Of course, I have told you as much as nothing and have spoken more with myself than to you.

I am very glad that you dedicate yourself increasingly to poetry. Our age has cast such a great burden of impressions on us that, as I feel daily more and more, only by way of sustained activity, continued through old age, and by way of serious, ever new attempts we can finally produce that which nature has determined as our destiny and which might have ripened perhaps faster though hardly as perfectly under different circumstances. If duties which are truly sacred to both of us call upon us, then we make a beautiful sacrifice to necessity by denying the love for the muses, at least for some time.

VI,341 | You must have had a happy evening when your comedy was performed and you felt yourself among the delighted spectators as the first moving force. Has it been printed, and can I purchase it in Frankfurt?

I wish your *Taschenbuch* a lot of happy collaborators. If you should be dissatisfied with the number of contributions and prefer to see the gap filled by me, then I will gladly dedicate to you another eight days, of course only in case of emergency; otherwise this would be presumptous for me to say. I soon will send you some poems of mine together with some contributions of another young poet. Those of Böhlendorff,[3] which I enclose, are presumably not without interest for your audience, and you can still make a selection if you see fit.

Be so good and make sure that the intervals which are left between the jambs in the manuscript of "Emilie" will be printed correctly.

Do not take offense because of the title; it would be necessary to write more prefaces than poems, and if with a few words I can quasi replace such a preface and signal to the reader that this is only a moment from Emilie's life and that the poet generally has to concentrate all biography as much as possible in a principal moment—why should I not?

As tentatively as I have written this sketch, I may still tell you that I am conscious of having said only little without dramatic or generally-poetic foundation.

Good night, my dear! My regards to HE. Steinkopf![4] In fact, to all my friends and acquaintances in Stuttgart, and do me the favor to write something about them, and write me again soon.

Hölderlin

No. 186   To Schelling[1]

My dear friend!

I have in the meantime participated in your cause and in your fame too loyally and too seriously as not allow myself once again to remind you of my existence.

| However, if I have meanwhile kept silence towards you, such was the case mainly because I hoped sometime to meet you—who always meant so much to me and who increased doing so—in a more significant position or at least in a manner worthy to remind you more fittingly of our friendship.

Now a request urges me to [write to] you earlier, and you will not mistake me in this appearance either. I have used the solitude in which I have been living here since last year to perhaps produce without distraction and with gathered and independent forces something more mature than has been the case thus far; and while I have already lived mostly for poetry, necessity and inclination did not allow me to move away from science so far as that I would not have sought to educate my convictions toward greater specificity and completeness and to attempt applying them as much as possible to the present and past world and [to observe the] effect. My thinking and my studies were mostly restricted to that which I practiced at first, poetry, insofar as it is living art and emerges simultaneously from genius, experience and reflection and is idealistic, systematic and individual. This led me to reflect about education and the drive toward education in general, about its cause and its determination, to the extent that it is idealistic and actively forming, and again to the extent that it works from the [point of] the ideal with a consiousness of its cause and of its own essence, and insofar as it works instinctively, yet according to its material as a drive of art and education, etc.

145

And I believed at the end of my investigations to have determined the perspective of so called humanity (to the extent that
it looks more onto the uniting and communal [element] in the
nature of human beings and their directions than onto the divid-
ing one which, to be sure, must be overlooked just as little)
firmer and more comprehensive than was known to me before.
These materials together inspired in me the conception of a
humanistic journal which, in its ordinary character, would be
practically poetic, then again also historically and philosophically
VI,347   instructive about poetry, finally | historically and philosophically
instructive from the viewpoint of humanity.

Forgive me for this ponderous preamble, my dear! Yet my
respect for you did not permit me to inform you of my project
so *ex abrupto*, and it seemed as though I owed you an account
of my activities, particularly because I might well be afraid that,
after my productions thus far, I no longer possessed the confidence which you once seemed to have in my philosophical and
poetic powers, now that I should have given you an example as
proof.

For you, who sees through and encompasses the nature of
man and his elements with this all too rare completeness and
flexibility, it will be easy to put yourself into my limited perspective and to sanction with your name and your participation
an enterprise which is designed to bring people closer to one
another *without insincerity and syncretism* by treating and urging
the individual forces, directions and connections of their nature
less strictly, yet which respectfully attempts to make intelligible
and sensible to these forces, directions and connections how they
are intrinsically and necessarily connected, and how each single
one of them may be contemplated in its excellence and purity
only in order to understand that it does nothing less than contradict another one—only provided that that [the other] one is
pure as well—but that each already contains within itself the
free demand for reciprocal effectiveness and harmonious alternation, and that the soul within the organic structure, which is
communal and proper to each member, does not leave alone any
individual one; that furthermore the soul cannot exist without
the organs and the organs not without the soul, and that they

both, if they exist separately and thus exist both in aorgic manner[2] must strive to organize themselves and must presuppose the organizing drive within themselves. I was hopefully entitled to say so by way of metaphor. It was to say nothing more than that immaterial (*stofflose*) genius could not exist without experience and that soulless experience could not exist without genius, but

VI,348   that they contain within themselves the necessity | to organize and constitute themselves through judgement and art, to coordinate themselves as a living, harmoniously alternating whole, so that finally the organizing art and the educating drive from which it emerges cannot exist and are not even conceivable without their inner element, the natural disposition, genius, nor without their external one, experience and historical learning.

I only wanted to touch for you on the most general character of the journal, that which is called its spirit. In my presentation and tone, I will attempt to be as universally intelligible as possible.

I did not consider it altogether proper to inform you more specifically about the plan which I had to develop for myself or about the materials which I have ready, as much as I was tempted—to the extent that such can be done based on the subject matter itself—to prove to you that my project is not done without foundations and sincerity, that it is perhaps more felicitous than my previous productions, and that, as much as I know and intuit your spirit and sense, I will not sin against you as regards [intellectual] tendency.

I will await your answer which I expect with hope and your views about the matter, in order to explain myself to you—should you ask me—more explicitly about the spirit and the conception of the journal to the extent that I was allowed to conceptualize it for myself, and to explain the potential and existing materials.

In any case, friend of my youth! Will you forgive me for having turned to you with old confidence and for having expressed the wish that, through your participation and company in this matter, you would sustain my courage which, in the meantime, has suffered manifold blows because of my situation and other circumstances, as I may probably confess to you. Through the greatest possible maturity of my own contributions and through the benevolent participation of merited writers, in which I take

VI,349

pride, I will do everything to lend to the journal the quality which it will need, so that you can answer for it to | your conscience and to the readership, [namely,] that you at least had lent your name and, if you could and would not give more, some contributions through the year.

The antiquarian Steinkopf in Stuttgart,[3] who has spoken to me willingly and understandingly about this matter and who, perhaps because he is a beginner, behaves for his part all the more reliably and loyally promises every contributor guaranteed pay; and I have made it a condition for him to send every collaborator at least one Karolin per page. If I already plan to live almost entirely for and on [the journal], I still do not believe to be entitled to ask for more for my person, since, as a writer, I have been basically without luck, and since my restricted life does not require any greater income. However, I left it to his gratitude and wisdom to make exceptions as he pleases for those collaborators where he wishes to do so.—Please excuse my talking also about this matter. Yet since it forms part of the issues, the situation is to blame that it cannot exist without such a pedant.

Be so kind, my dear! to please me soon at least with some answer, and believe [me] that I have respected as never before and do respect you ever more.[4]

Your
Hölderlin

P.S. My publisher unites his request expressly with mine.
My address is: at the glazier Wagner, resident at Homburg near Frankfurt.

No. 236   To Casimir Ulrich Böhlendorff[1]

Nürtingen, near Stuttgart, December 4, 1801

My dear Böhlendorff

Your kind words and your presence in them have made me very happy.

Your *Fernando* has alleviated my bosom a good deal. The progress of my friends is such a good sign to me. We have one destiny. If one is making progress, then the other will not be left behind either.[2]

My dear friend! You have gained so much in precision and effective flexibility and did not lose anything in warmth; on the contrary, like a good blade, the flexibility of your spirit has proven all the stronger in the humbling school. This is what I congratulate you on above all. We learn nothing with more difficulty than to freely use the national. And, I believe that it is precisely the clarity of the | presentation that is so natural to us as is for the Greeks the fire from heaven. For exactly that reason they will have to be surpassed in beautiful passion—which you have also preserved for yourself—rather than in that Homeric presence of mind and talent for presentation.

It sounds paradoxical. Yet I argue it once again and leave it for your examinatioin and use: in the progress of education the truly national will become the ever less attractive. Hence the Greeks are less master of the sacred pathos, because to them it was inborn, whereas they excel in their talent for presentation, beginning with Homer, because this exceptional man was sufficiently sensitive to conquer the Western *Junonian sobriety* for his Appolonian empire and thus to veritably appropriate what is foreign.

With us it is the reverse. Hence it is also so dangerous to deduce the rules of art for oneself exclusively from Greek excellence. I have labored long over this and know by now that, with the exception of what must be the highest for the Greeks and for us—namely, the living relationship and destiny—we must not share anything identical with them.

Yet what is familiar must be learned as well as what is alien. This is why the Greeks are so indispensable for us. It is only that we will not follow them in our own, national [spirit] since, as I said, the *free* use of *what is one's own* is the most difficult.

It seems to me that your good genius has inspired you to treat the drama in a more epic manner. It is, overall, an authentic modern tragedy. For this is the tragic to us: that, packed up in any container, we very quietly move away from the realm of the living, [and] not that—consumed in flames—we expiate the flames which we could not tame.

And indeed! The former moves the innermost soul just as well as the latter. It is not such an impressive, yet a more profound destiny, and a noble soul guides also such a dying [man] with fear and empathy and holds up the spirit amidst wreath. The great Jupiter, | then, is after all the last thought during the death of a mortal being—whether he die according to our or ancient destiny—if the poet has depicted this dying, as he should and as you visibly intended and achieved in the whole and particularly in some masterful moves.

VI,427

> "A narrow path leads into an unlit vale
> Forced down there by treachery."

and elsewhere.—You are on a good path, stay with it. However, I will study your *Fernando* with care and take it to heart and then perhaps tell you something more interesting about it. In no case enough!

About myself and how I have been thus far, how far I have stayed worthy of you and my friends, also what I am engaged in and what I will produce, as little as it is, about all that I will write to you next time from the neighbourhood of your Spain,[3] namely from Bordeaux where I will travel next week as a private tutor and preacher in a German-Protestant household. I will have to keep my wits about me: in France, in Paris; I look forward to the sight of the ocean [and] also of the sun in the Provence.

O friend! The world lies ahead of me brighter than usual and more serious. Yes! It pleases me how it works, pleases me as when, in the summer, "the old holy father pours down lightnings with calm hand out of red clouds."[4] For among everything that I can see of God this sign has become my chosen one. At other times, I could jubilate about a new truth, an improved outlook on what is above us and around us; now I fear that I might end like the old Tantalus who received more from the Gods than he could take.

Yet I do whatever I can, as well as I can, and think, when seeing others, how on my path I also must go where they go, think that it is godless and mad to search for a path which was safe of all attack, and that there is no remedy against death.

And now, farewell my dear friend! Until soon. I am now full of parting. I have not wept for so long. Yet it has cost me bitter | tears when I decided to leave my fatherland so late, perhaps forever. For what more precious thing do I have in this world? But they cannot make use of me. I will and must stay German, even if necessity of my heart and need for food were to drive me to Otaheiti.[5]

My regards to our Muhrbeck.[6] How is he? He surely is doing fine. He will remain there for us. Forgive my ingratitude. I had recognized you, I saw you, yet only through yellow glasses. I would have to tell you so much, you good people! You probably for me, too. Where will you stay in the future, my Böhlendorff? Well, those are small matters. If you write to me, send the letter to the merchant Landauer[7] in Stuttgart. He will definitely forward it to me. Also, send me your address.

Your

H.

1,428

No. 240   To Casimir Ulrich Böhlendorff[1]

My dear friend!

I have not written you for a long time, have been meanwhile in France and have seen the sad, solitary earth, the shepherds of Southern France and individual beauties, men and women, who have grown up in the anxiety of patriotic doubt and hunger.

The tremendous element, the fire of the sky and the silence of the people, their life within nature, and their limitedness and satisfaction has continually affected me, and as it is said of the heroes, so I may say that Apollo has struck me.

In the areas which border to the Vendée,[2] I have been interested in the wild, the martial [character], the purely male for which the light of life becomes immediate in eyes and limbs and which, in the intimation of death, feels like a [moment of] virtuosity, and which fulfills its thirst for knowledge.

The athletic [character] of the southern people in the ruins of the ancient spirit made me more familiar with the specific essence of the Greeks; I became acquainted with their nature and their wisdom, their body, the way in which they grew within their climate, and the rule by which they protected their exuberant genius against the violence of the elements.

This determined their popularity, their habit to assume a foreign character and communicate themselves through them; hence they possess their individually-proper [character] which appears alive to the extent that supreme understanding is, in the Greek sense, reflexive power; and this becomes intelligible for us if we comprehend the heroic body of the Greeks; [reflexive power] is tenderness, like our popularity.

Beholding the ancients has given me an impression which renders intelligible to me not only the Greeks but, generally, the highest in art which, even in the highest movement and phenomenalization of the concepts and of everything that is

√I,433   meant seriously, nevertheless sustains | everything upright and for itself, so that security of this sense is the supreme form of the sign.

After several shocks and turmoils of the soul, it was necessary for me to settle down for some time, and I live meanwhile in my home town.[3]

The more I study it, the more forcefully the nature of my country seizes me. The thunderstorm, not only in its highest manifestation but, precisely in this sense as force and appearance among other forms of the sky; the light in its effects, forming nationally and as a principle and mode of destiny—that something be sacred to us—its force in coming and going; the characteristic element of the woods and the coinciding of various characters of nature in one area; that all sacred places of the earth are gathered around one place, and the philosophical light around my window: they are now my delight; may I remember how I have come to this point.

My dear friend! I think that we will not comment [on] the poets up to our time, but that the form of poetry (*Sangart*) in general will take a different character, and that therefore we do not succeed because, since the Greeks, we have again begun to poeticize in patriotic natural, and in properly original manner.

If you would just write to me soon. I need your pure tone. The psyche among friends, the origination of thoughts in conversation and correspondence is necessary for artists. Otherwise we have nobody for ourselves, but he belongs to the sacred image which we produce. Farewell

Your

H.

The Oldest System-Program of German Idealism[1]

[. . .] an ethics. Since all metaphysics will eventually be collapsed into morals (for which Kant, with his two practical postulates, has given an example, yet which he has not exhausted), this ethics will be nothing else but a complete system of all ideas or, which is the same, of all practical postulates. The first idea, of course, is the representation of myself as an absolutely free being. Simultaneously with the free, self-conscious being, there emerges an entire world—from out of nothing—the only true and conceivable creation *out of nothing*—[.] From here I will descend to the regions of physics; the question is this: how must a world for a moral being be constituted? I would like to once again lend wings to our slow physics which has been moving so laboriously by way of experimentation.

Thus—when philosophy provides the ideas [and] experience the data, we can finally achieve a physics on a large scale which I expect from future epochs. It does not seem that present physics can satisfy a creative spirit as ours is or should be.

From nature I move on to man's works. Beginning with the idea of humanity—I want to demonstrate that there does not exist any idea of the state, because the state is something mechanical, just as there is no idea of a machine. Only that which is object of freedom is called idea. Hence, we must also move beyond the state!—For every state must treat free human beings

like a mechanical set of wheels; | and that it must not; therefore, it shall cease to exist. You see yourself that all ideas here, of eternal peace, etc., are only ideas *subordinated* to a higher idea. At the same time, I want to establish here the principles for a *history of humanity* and to strip the entire miserable human construct of state, constitution, government, legislation—down to its very skin. Finally, the ideas of a moral world, divinity, immortality—overthrow of all superstition, persecution of the priesthood which has recently feigned reason, by way of reason itself.—Absolute freedom of all spirits who carry the intellectual world within themselves, and who must search neither God nor immortality *outside of themselves.*

Finally the idea which unites all [previous ones], the idea of beauty, the word understood in the higher, Platonic sense. I am convinced now, that the highest act of reason, which—in that it comprises all ideas—is an aesthetic act, and that *truth and goodness* are united as sisters *only in beauty.* The philosopher must possess as much aesthetic capacity as the poet. The people without an aesthetic sensibility are our philosophical literalists.[2] Philosophy of the spirit is an aesthetic philosophy. One cannot be full of spirit, one cannot even reason about history with wit and spirit—without an aesthetic sensibility. Here, it shall become manifest what the people actually lack who do not understand any ideas,—and who are sufficiently open-hearted to admit that everything is dark for them as soon as it moves beyond tables and calculations.

Thus poetry achieves a higher dignity, she becomes again in the end what she was in the beginning—*teacher of humanity*; for there no longer exists any philosophy, any history; poetry alone will survive all other sciences and arts.

At the same time, we hear so frequently that the masses need a religion of the senses. Not only the masses but the philosopher, too, is in need of it. Monotheism of reason and of the heart, polytheism of the imagination and art, those are what we need!

First, I will speak here of an idea which, as far as I know, | has not occurred to anyone—[.] We need a new mythology, however, this mythology must be at the service of the ideas, it must become a mythology of reason.

Until we render the ideas aesthetic, that is, mythological, they will not be of any interest to the populace, and vice versa: until mythology has become reasonable, the philosopher has to be ashamed of it. Thus the enlightened and the unenlightened finally have to shake hands; mythology must become philosophical in order to make the people reasonable, and philosophy must turn mythological in order to make the philosophers sensuous. Then there prevails eternal unity among us. No longer the contemptuous look, no longer the blind trembling of the populace before its sages and priests. Then only awaits us the equal cultivation of all powers, of the individual as well as of all individuals. No power will be suppressed any longer, then there prevails universal freedom and equality of the spirits!—A higher spirit, sent from heavens, will have to found this new religion among us; it will be the last, the greatest achievement of mankind.

Notes

Introduction

1. For some translations of Hölderlin's writings, see the bibliography, especially the entries J. Adler and T. Bahti. All references to primary philosophical texts as well as to secondary writings on Hölderlin can be found in the bibliography below.

2. As examples of this discussion, see Paul de Man's "The Image of Rousseau in the Poetry of Hölderlin," "Wordsworth and Hölderlin," or Stanley Corngold's "Hölderlin and the Interpretation of the Self." The first one to include Hölderlin's theoretical writings in the discussion of problems in contemporary critical theory appears to be Andrzej Warminski, *Readings in Interpretation: Hölderlin, Hegel and Heidegger*. (Minneapolis: University of Minnesota Press, 1987)

3. Ernst Cassirer, *The Philosophy of the Enlightenment*. Boston: Beacon, 1955, p. 9.

4. "Semper igitur praedicatum seu consequens inest subjecto seu antecedenti. et in hoc ipso consistit natura veritatis . . ." G. W. Leibniz, "Primae Veritates" *Opuscules* (et Fragments Inédits), Ed. Louis Couturat, (Hildesheim: Georg Olms. [1903], 1961), p. 518.

5. Cf. Leibniz's treatise on "Vérités Nécessaires et Contingentes," ibid., 16ff.

6. Cf. Ernst Cassirer, *Das Erkenntnisproblem*. [1903]. (Darmstadt: Wissenschaftliche Buchgesellschaft, 1977), vol. II, 142f., 180.

7. Cassirer, *The Philosophy of Enlightenment*, op.cit., 32.

8. Pajanotis Kondylis, *Aufklärung*. Stuttgart: Klett-Cotta, 1981, p. 21.

9. The relation between the realm of the sensuous and the concept of intuition is, of course, very complex. In the following, I use the term "intuition" in an iconic sense which the German frequently

renders as *Bild-Anschauung*. Since Leibniz, such an intuition had been
a product of the imagination "without a consciousness of [its] reason."
See, F. Kaulbach, "Anschauung." *Historisches Wörterbuch der Philosophie.* Ed. Joachim Ritter et al. (Stuttgart: Schwabe & Co., 1971). vol. I,
340 ff.

10. For this aspect of pre-Kantian aesthetics, see Alfred Bäumler's
discussion of Baumgarten's *Reflections on Poetry* and *Aesthetica*, in *Das
Irrationalitätsproblem in der Aesthetik des 18. Jahrhunderts.* [1923].
(Darmstadt: Wissenschaftliche Buchgesellschaft, 1967), 207 ff.

11. According to Kant, the beautiful as a symbol of morality can
only share "the form of reflection" but not the content with that which
it represents; thus he discriminates sharply between the respective
semiologies of reason and intuition: "The intuitive in cognition must
be opposed to the discursive (not to the symbolical). The former is
either *schematical,* by *demonstration,* or *symbolical,* as a representation
in accordance with a mere *analogy.*" *Critique of Judgment,* p. 197 [B
256].

12. Bäumler, op. cit., 353.

13. cf. Kondylis, op. cit., 563 ff.

14. cf. ibid., 580.

15. See Ernst Cassirer, *The Platonic Renaissance in England.* Trans.
James P. Pettegrove. (Austin: Texas Univ. Press, 1953), who discusses
the disruptive impact of the Platonic concept of *eros* on the dominating
philosophy of Empiricism.

16. ". . . que le désire de l'âme est une tendence vers l'union
parfaite et intime avec l'essence de l'objet désiré;" Hemsterhuis, *Oeuvres
Philosophiques,* 56 (translation mine).

17. "En vérité, tout ce qui est visible ou sensible pour nous, tend
vers l'unité ou vers l'union. Pourtant tout est composé d'individus
absolument isolés; et nonobstant cette belle apparance d'une chaine
d'êtres etroitement liés, il paroît clair que chaque individu existe pour
exister, et non pour l'existence d'un autre" Hemsterhuis, ibid., 67
(translation mine).

18. See the discussion of Hemsterhuis by Gerhard Kurz, *Mittelbarkeit und Vereinigung,* 19 ff., and by Dieter Henrich, *Hegel im Kontext,*
12 ff. The simultaneous reference toward self and other implied by
Hemsterhuis' conception of *eros* already contains the seed for Fichte's

notion of "reciprocal determination" and "striving" in the *Science of Knowledge.*

19. Herder's is essentially concerned with securing the status of the individual against the seemingly all-devouring nature of "love." Thus he seeks to privilege "friendship" over "love." "We are individual beings, and we must be such if we do not mean to abandon the ground of all delight, our own consciousness in the course of delight, and to lose ourselves, in order to find ourselves in another being which we ultimately never are and which we never can become." *Liebe und Selbstheit,* p. 321, (translation mine).

20. "Thus love, for him, changes into a force which is to be thought not as a state but only as a movement through opposites. It becomes a principle of history. (. . .) Thus the historical course of man is also threatened by manifold errors. Hölderlin applies to it the metaphor of a path—an excentric path." Dieter Henrich, *Hegel im Kontext,* 17, (translation mine). For the concept of the "excentric path," see also the essay by Marshall Brown.

21. On the general question of aesthetics and their relation to reason, see Alfred Bäumler, *Das Irrationalitätsproblem,* and Cassirer, op. cit., 275 ff.

22. On Hölderlin's early Kant reception, see Ernst Müller who provides useful information on the Swabian theologians Boek and Flatt and their attempts to to appropriate Kant's philosophy for religious argumentation. *Hölderlin: Studien zur Geschichte seines Geistes,* 88 ff.

23. *Early Theological Writings,* 224ff. and 302ff. (Nohl, Theologische Jugendschriften, 276ff. and 377ff.). Of interest here is also Lukacs' interpretation of these texts. As Lukacs argues, Hegel does not see love as the ultimate stratum of reconciliation. "Thus what love lacks according to Hegel is objectivity. It is one manifestation of the divine principle in man, but it is not able to create a living relationship between subject and object." *The Young Hegel,* Trans. Rodney Livingstone, (Cambridge: MIT Press, 1975), p. 187.

24. The influence of Schiller on the young Hölderlin was, of course, considerable. Apart from Schiller's significant contribution to the publication of *Hyperion* and to providing Hölderlin with a tutoring position in Jena, Hölderlin also felt greatly inclined to share his philosophical reflections with the by then well-established poet. In close relation to the three fragments discussed here, Hölderlin writes to Schiller on September 4, 1795: "The displeasure with myself and that

which surrounds me has driven me into abstraction; I attempt to develop for myself the idea of an infinite progress of philosophy [and] to show that the relentless condition to be posited to every philosophical system, [namely] the union of the subject and the object in an absolute "I" or however one wants to call it,—is indeed possible aesthetically in intellectual intuition, theoretically however only as an infinite approximation, like the approximation of the square to the circle." Letter No. 104 (*SE: VI*, 181). See also Hölderlin's letter to Niethammer, No. 117 (translated below).

25. Letter No. 88, Oct. 10th, 1794 (*SE: VI*, 137).

26. Letter No. 89, Nov. 1794. "Fichte is now the soul of Jena. Thank God! that he is. A man of such depth and energy of spirit I have not known elsewhere." (*SE: VI*, 139)

27. For the difficulties of dating the last of Hölderlin's three early essays, "Judgment and Being," see Dieter Henrich, "Hölderlin über Urteil und Sein."

28. See Martin Heidegger, *Kant and the Problem of Metaphysics.* Trans. James S. Churchill. (Bloomington: Indiana Univ. Press, 1962). 138f. "The imagination forms in advance, and before all experience of the essent, the aspect of the horizon of objectivity as such. This formation of the aspect in the pure form [*Bild*] of time not only precedes this or that experience of the essent but is also prior to any such possible experience. In offering a pure aspect in this way, the imagination is in no case and in no wise dependent on the presence of an essent. It is so far from being thus dependent that its pre-formation of a pure schema, for example, substance (permanence), consists in bringing into view something on the order of constant presence [*ständige Anwesenheit*]. It is only in the horizon of this presence that this or that 'presence of an object' can reveal itself." Heidegger's incisive interpretation shows how Kant grew increasingly uncomfortable with the idea that the coherence and systematicity of the presupposed realm of experience was contingent on the imagination's "transcendental synthesis" itself.

29. In light of Hölderlin's subsequent remarks in this and the other two early essays, it would be reductive to consider his claims about the "unity of the manifold" a mere misconception of Kant. For a thorough, although somewhat over-contextualized interpretation of Hölderlin's first two essays, "On the Law of Freedom" and "On the Concept of Punishment," see F. Strack, *Aesthetik und Freiheit.*

30. As F. Strack has shown, Hölderlin moves beyond Kant's conception of art as a non-conceptual analogue of Reason itself: "The imagination (as a productive faculty of cognition) is very powerful in creating another nature, as it were out of the material the actual nature gives it. And by an aesthetical idea, I understand that representation of the imagination which occasions much thought, without however any definite thought, i.e., any *concept*, being capable of being adequate of it; (. . .) Such representations of the imagination we may call *ideas*, partly because they at least strive after something which lies beyond the boundaries of experience and so seek to approximate to a presentation of concepts of reason (intellectual ideas) . . ." *Critique of Judgment*, 157 [B 193]. See also, F. Strack, op. cit., 57ff.

31. cf. *Critique of Judgment*, 205 ff. [A 266 ff.].

32. See F. Strack, op. cit., who points out that the concept of "intellectual intuition" is about to emerge in this fragment. op. cit., 65.

33. "The consciousness of this fundamental law may be called a fact of reason, since one cannot ferret it out from antecedent data of reason, such as the consciousness of freedom, (for this is not antecedently given), and since it forces itself upon us as a synthetic proposition a priori based on no pure or empirical intuition. It would be analytic if the freedom of the will were presupposed, but for this, as a positive concept, an intellectual intuition would be needed, and here we cannot assume it." *Critique of Practical Reason*, 31 [A 56, 57].

34. "Before reason awoke, there was as yet neither commandment nor prohibition and hence also no violation of either. But when reason began to set about its business, it came, in all its pristine weakness, into conflict with animality, with all its power. (. . .) Morally, the step from this latter state was therefore a fall; physically, it was a punishment, for a whole host of formerly unknown ills were a consequence of this fall. The history of nature therefore begins with good, for it is the work of God, while the history of freedom begins with wickedness, for it is the work of man." Immanuel Kant, "Conjectural Beginning of Human History," p. 61 [A 13].

35. The distinction seems to echo that of Fichte between a "real cause" and an "ideal cause," made in the *Science of Knowledge*, 145–147. However, already Kant states in the "Preface" to the *Critique of Practical Reason* that "I will only remind the reader that, though freedom is certainly the *ratio essendi* of the moral law, the latter is the *ratio*

cognoscendi of freedom." p. 4, note 1 [A 6]. See also F. Strack (op. cit., 155ff.) who, however, fails to see the implications which Hölderlin's introduction of the "accidental" has for the general problematic of grounding philosophy as the systematization of difference.

36. It should be noted that Hölderlin speaks of punishment as a quasi-ontological *ratio cognoscendi* for the metaphysical conception of order, the "law." By contrast, Kant speaks of "something else in the idea of our practical reason which accompanies transgression of a moral law, namely its culpability [*Strafwürdigkeit*]." *Critique of Practical Reason*, 39 [A 65]. By restricting the discussion of punishment to that of "culpability," Kant already presupposes the recognizability of a transgression as such, whereas for Hölderlin the phenomenality of punishment itself is precisely what still needs to be established.

37. See Henrich, *Hegel im Kontext*, 12, who also notes that "Hölderlin, in the aftermath of Kant's doctrine of freedom, was the first to contest Kant's thesis that the supreme point from which philosophy ought to proceed be the unity of a consciousness of the "I" as the subject of thinking."

38. op. cit., 167 ff.

39. Letter No. 97, translated below. More than any other letter, this one evidences Fichte's influence on Hölderlin's view concerning the transcendental problem of morality and freedom.

40. Henrich, "Hölderlin über Urteil und Sein," 77 ff.

41. "The proposition 'A = A' constitutes a judgment. But all judgment, so empirical consciousness tells us, is an activity of the human mind. (. . .) The self's positing of itself is thus its own pure activity." Shortly afterwards, Fichte reiterates this postulate: "And this now makes it perfectly clear in what sense we are using the word 'I' in this context, and leads us to an exact account of the self as absolute subject. *That whose being or essence consists simply in the fact that it posits itself as existing*, is the self as absolute subject." J. G. Fichte, *Science of Knowledge*, 97f.

42. It is surprising that interpreters of Fichte still commit the error of such a reification of Fichte's postulate, such as when Dieter Henrich argues that "to speak of an 'I' is only sensible if one refers it to self-consciousness." *Hegel im Kontext*, 21.

43. "Die Setzung des A identisch mit sich selbst bedeutet die Selbstbehauptung der grundlegenden Relation, in der sich die Erkenntnis

des A konstituiert, durch alle Mannigfaltigkeit der möglichen Zeit-punkte und möglichen Anwendungsfälle hindurch. Dass ein bestimmter Inhalt mit sich selbst identisch 'ist', bedeutet, dass er als solcher *rekog-noszierbar* ist: und diese Rekognition vermag niemals die blosse 'Wahr-nehmung', sondern lediglich eine Anschauung zu leisten, die die Unendlichkeit und Totalität aller möglichen Wahrnehmungen umfasst." Ernst Cassirer, *Das Erkenntnisproblem*, [1920] (Darmstadt: Wissenschaf-tliche Buchgesellschaft, 1974), vol. III, 141f. (translation mine).

44. "Denn das Ich, von dem hier die Rede ist, ist kein isolierter oder isolierbarer Teil des Seins; ist in diesem Sinne nicht blosse 'Sub-jektivität', sondern ursprüngliche Identität des Subjektiven und Objek-tiven." Cassirer, ibid., 149.

45. cf. Cassirer, ibid., 151.

46. Discussing Fichte's lectures, Hölderlin writes in a letter to Hegel (No. 94, Jan 26, 1795) where he discusses Fichte's lectures: Fichte "wants to move in theory beyond the fact of consciousness; many of his statements show that, and that is just as certain and even more strikingly transcendent than if the metaphysicians so far would move beyond the existence of the world—his absolute 'I' (Spinoza's Sub-stance) contains all reality; it is everything, and outside of it there is nothing; hence there is no object for this 'I', for otherwise not all reality would be within it; however, a consciousness without object cannot be thought, . . ." The conflation of the absolute 'I' with an anthro-pomorphic notion of consciousness would have indeed justified Höld-erlin's initial suspicion that Fichte was prone to "dogmatism." However, Fichte, who had to contend with such charges throughout his career, was quite conscious of this problematic when he ridiculed the readers of his *Science of Knowledge* who wanted to convert the "intelligible" relation into a realistic narrative, into the "biography of man prior to his birth." Quoted in Cassirer, op. cit., 164.

47. Already in his dissertation, *De Mundi Sensibilis atque Intelli-gibilis Forma et Principiis* (*Werkausgabe*, vol. V, ed. W. Weisschedel, Frankfurt: Suhrkamp, 1977 [A_2 12]), Kant states that there cannot be anything like an intellectual intuition.

48. Nicolai de Cusa, *Trialogus de Possest*, ed. R. Steiger, (Ham-burg: Felix Meiner, 1973), p. 45.

49. "Felicitas enim ultima, quae est visio intellectualis ipsius cunctipotentis, est adimpletio illius desiderii nostri, quo omnes scire

desideramus, nisi igitur ad scientiam Dei, qua mundum creavit, per-
venerimus, non quietatur spiritus." ibid., 45f.

50. "There exists, then, an obscure or *clear* cognition, and the
clear one is eventually confuse or *distinct*, and the distinct one is either
inadequate or *adequate*, which is either symbolical or *intuitive*." "Med-
itationes de Cognitione, Veritate et Ideis," G. W. Leibniz, *Die Philo-
sophischen Schriften*, ed. C. J. Gerhardt, [1880] (Hildesheim: Georg
Olms, 1960), vol. IV, 422ff. ˙(translation mine).

51. "If indeed all which is implicit in a distinct notion has ret-
roactively become distinctly known (. . .) the cognition is adequate,
[yet] I do not know whether man can give a perfect example of it."
ibid., 423 (translation mine).

52. "Et certe cum notio valde composita est, non possumus omnes
ingredientes eam notiones simul cogitare: ubi tamen hoc licet, vel
saltem in quantum licet, cognitionem voco *intuitivam*." ibid., 423
(translation mine).

53. "Meanwhile nothing is more true than that we have an idea
of God, and that the most perfect Being is possible, indeed necessary."
ibid., 424 (translation mine).

54. See J. G. Fichte, *Gesamtausgabe* I,2. 57, where he applies
the concept of an "intellectual intuition" for the first time.

55. Fichte, "Second Introduction" to the *Science of Knowledge*,
41.

56. ibid., 38

57. ibid., 40

58. "How, that is, can it be established beyond doubt that such
an intuition does not rest upon a purely subjective deception, if it
possesses no objectivity that is universal and acknowledged by all men?
This universally acknowledged and altogether incontestable objectivity
of intellectual intuition is art itself. For the aesthetic intuition simply
is the intellectual intuition become objective." *System of Transcendental
Idealism*, 229 [German, 625]. Schelling's position eventually culminates
in his *Philosophie der Kunst*, thus representing the most systematic artic-
ulation of that idea.

59. See especially Martin Heidegger's interpretation of Hegel as
the culminating point of German Idealism: "Demanded by the guiding
and grounding problem of Western philosophy, Hegel's *Phenomenology
of Spirit* is the self-presentation of *reason* which in German Idealism is

recognized as an absolute one, and which is understood by Hegel as spirit." Martin Heidegger, *Hegel's Phänomenologie des Geistes*, Frankfurt: Klostermann, 1980; p. 59 (translation mine).

60. Else Buddeberg, "Hölderlins Begriff der 'Rezeptivität des Stoffes'," 182. Buddeberg's astute analysis shows how Hölderlin's conception of the aesthetic moves away from the philosophical systems of Kant and Fichte toward a conception of intellectual intuition which is "fundamentally guided by the Platonic *anamnesis*." ibid., 176.

61. See Leonardus van de Velde, who points out how Hölderlin, in his conception of the "poetic spirit" retains and even radicalizes the idea of difference. *Herrschaft und Knechtschaft bei Hölderlin*, 253 ff.

62. Among the essays which have not been included in this translation are Hölderlin's excerpts from "Jacobi's letters on the doctrine of Spinoza" (*SE*: IV, 207–210), his essay "A word on the *Iliad*," whose argument is presented more amply in the subsequent "On the Different Forms of Poetic Composition" and some very brief fragments which thus far have received little or no critical attention.

On the Law of Freedom

1. According to Beissner, (*SE*: IV, 400f.), orthographic peculiarities indicate that the text, which breaks off after two pages, was written no later than November 1794.

On the Concept of Punishment

1. The text dates from around February 1795, (cf. *SE*: IV, 402).

2. This parenthetical reminder suggests that Hölderlin did not conceive of this text as the final version.

3. Hölderlin's distinction between *Erkenntnisgrund* and *Realgrund* seems close to that made by Fichte in the *Science of Knowledge* (pp. 147 ff.). However, the second term in Fichte's work, with which Hölderlin was certainly familiar, is *Idealgrund*. It is thus possible that Hölderlin reinstates the Kantian distinction between the law as the *ratio cognoscendi* for freedom and, conversely, freedom as the *ratio essendi* of the law. cf. *Critique of Practical Reason*, 4 [German: A 6]. However, Hölderlin alters Kant's position on "culpability" markedly (cf. *ibid.*, 39 ff.

[German: A 66, 67]). For a discussion of the intellectual background of Hölderlin's early theoretical writings, see F. Strack, *Aesthetik und Freiheit*, 161 ff.

Judgment and Being

1. The text appears to have been written early in 1795. For a long interpretative and philological assessment of this, perhaps most significant, fragment of the "early" Hölderlin, see: Dieter Henrich, "Hölderlin über "Urteil und Sein".—Hölderlin stresses the etymology of the German *Urteil* ("Ur-theil") by pointing to its implication of an "arche-separation".

2. The syntax in the MS is somewhat cryptic, however, the completion of the phrase appears quite unambiguous.

The Perspective from which We Have to Look at Antiquity

1. According to the *FE* (vol. 14, 83), this essay (whose draft-character is evidenced by the abbreviated *per procura* in 1. 1) was written after Hölderlin had completed his idyll "Emilie vor ihrem Brauttag." The letter to Neuffer from July 3, 1799 (see below) contains clear resonances of the language and ideas in this essay.

2. The following, bracketed < > passage is emphasized in the *SE* by way of an extra-wide script. In the original MS., Hölderlin underlines the entire passage and doubly underlines the concluding passage on p. 222 (*SE*); see also, *FE* (vol. 14, pp. 88f.).

On the Different Forms of Poetic Composition

1. Based on the paper used by Hölderlin, this essay as, well as its shorter first version "A word on the Iliad," cannot be dated earlier than July 1799 (cf. *FE*: vol. 14, 97).

2. Two pages are missing in the MS. In his related text, "A word on the Iliad" (*SE*: IV, 226–27), Hölderlin continues his characterization of the natural (naive) type with that of the "heroic" and "ideal" one.

Beissner (*SE*: IV, 747) speculates that this description filled the missing two pages.

3. Hölderlin refers to and quotes from Johann Heinrich Voss' hexametric translation of the *Iliad* which had appeared in 1793, following Voss' earlier translation of the *Odysee* from 1781.

Reflection

1. This text is published in the *FE* (vol. 14, 51–71) under the title "Seven Maxims." The editors of the *FE* date the text around Spring 1799. Hölderlin's experimentation with aphorisms here seems to be indebted to Novalis' *Blütenstaub* and to the first two pieces of Schlegel's *Atheneaum* (May and July, 1798).

2. This short paragraph remains in terminology and argument rather undeveloped and, as a result, has not yet received any critical attention. Beissner's suggestion (*SE*: IV, 408) that the ideas may be related to a passage in Herder, (*Werke*, Suphan, I, 192–96) needs yet to be explored in its implications.

3. This sentence must be read as an antithetical completion of the previous paragraph, and it contains no independent predicate.

"The Sages, however . . ."

1. To be dated around April 1799 (cf. *FE*: vol. 14, 73), this text might be understood as a critical statement against Schelling's seeming Spinozism, specifically against his non-reflective and somewhat monistic conception of the Absolute. Hölderlin may be seen to anticipate Hegel's later critique of Schelling in the "Preface" to the *Phenomenology of Spirit*.

The Ground for Empedocles

1. Together with the essay "Becoming in Decline," this long theoretical text belongs to the last works of the Homburg period, and it cannot have been composed before August/September 1799 (cf. *SE*: IV, 371).

2. At least two pages from the folio are lost here, yet according to Beissner, the text had originally been completed (*SE*: IV, 701). The preserved text resumes with a long fragmentary sentence.

3. The translation of Hölderlin's distinction between *organisch* and *aorgisch* and the translation of *aorgisch* as "aorgic" requires some explanation. Hölderlin's distinction must be understood in the context of Swabian Pietism and the energetically inspired concept of nature of German Romanticism. Unlike Schelling's distinction between *organisch* and *anorganisch*, Hölderlin's "organic" implies not a natural organism or the like, but designates the organized, reflected principle of the spirit and of art. Similarly, the term *aorgisch*, subsequently translated as "aorgic," does not refer to the merely lifeless but designates, in the course of this translation, the unreflexive, unrepresented, disorganizing manifestation of nature. The fate of Empedocles is connected to the progressive harmonization of this bipolarity. For a brief historical account of this early idealist opposition, from Hölderlin through Goethe and Schelling, see *Historisches Wörterbuch der Philosophie*, ed. Joachim Ritter (Basel, Stuttgart: Schwabe & Co., 1971–) [vol. 6, 1329.]

4. Translation of *Bildungstriebe und Bildungskräfte*. These terms have an important operative function for the overall determination of the initially "alien subject-matter." See Gerhard Kurz, *Mittelbarkeit und Vereinigung*, 118ff.

5. Hölderlin's seemingly idiosyncratic image of Empedocles as a son of his "heaven" actually echos Winckelmann's explanation of the exemplary status of Greek art by the "temperate" character of the Greek people, something he attributes to their moderate climate. See Peter Szondi's discussion of the respective passage from Winckelmann in *Poetik und Geschichtsphilosophie*, vol. I, 26ff.

6. Hölderlin's neologism *Bildsamkeit* is translated here as "formative capacity." Unfortunately, the visual connotation of the noun *Bild* is lost. In general, it should be kept in mind that also the German word *Bildung* connotes such an iconic quality.

On the Process of the Poetic Spirit

1. To be dated around the first half of 1800, toward the end of the Homburg period, this sketch serves the purpose of Hölderlin's theoretical self-definition rather than addressing a distinctive audience. The frequently very complex sentence structure reflects the tentative

character of this essay which nevertheless remains Hölderlin's longest complete prose piece. See also, *FE*: vol. 14, p. 179.

2. Strictly speaking, this is where Hölderlin ends his first sentence. However, the hyperbolic construction that began with "Once he has realized . . ." is continued.

3. Hölderlin's use of the term "sphere" here is used in a manner very similar to Fichte who develops this concept in his *Science of Knowledge* (1794/95), 175ff. Indeed, Fichte's text may be read with good reason as both, a methodological and conceptual dictionary for Hölderlin's Homburg writings.

4. The German distinction is made more explicitly than can be rendered here. However, it should be noted that each of the three concepts, "the ideal, life and the individual" ("Idealisches, Lebendiges und Individuelles") opposes itself and not one of the other two.

5. The pronoun "it," which recurs as the subject in the following sentences, refers to "significance" which, out of "foundation and significance" (see beginning of paragraph), appears to have been given more emphasis.

6. The pronoun "it" refers to the "poetic individuality" which Hölderlin had begun to define above and whose definition is continued throughout this paragraph.

7. Hölderlin's explication of the relation between the 'I' and what he refers to as "subjective nature" is based on a tripartite distinction between different aspects of cognition; the threefold distinction between *Erkenntnis / Erkanntes / Erkennendes Ich* is translated as "cognition / cognized / cognizing 'I'."

8. The term *Ahndung*—18th Century spelling for modern high-German *Ahnung*—assumes a crucial function here and below in Hölderlin's section on poetic language. Ordinarily used in the sense of a "presentiment" (cf. Grimm, *Wörterbuch*), the term here acquires a function analogous to that of reason. Although he rejects *Ahndung* as a mental delusion, namely, because it implies foreknowledge, Kant also observes on its connotation of remembrance: "*Ahnden* is equivalent to 'keep something in mind' [*Gedenken*]. Used with the dative it means that something presents itself vaguely to my mind. Used with the accusative it means to remember someone's deed with malicious intention (that is, to punish). It is always the same notion only used in different ways." *Anthropology from a Pragmatic Point of View*, Trans. Victor Lyle Dowdell. (Carbondale & Edwardsville: Southern Illinois

Univ. Press, 1978), p. 78. Hölderlin mediates the potentially mysti-
fying connotations of such foreknowledge by showing how "cognition
intuits language" *only after* a reflective process in which the "primordial,
living sensation [. . .] has been purified and reflected." For the intricate
and very suggestive function of the term, see especially the article by
W. Nieke in *Historisches Wörterbuch der Philosophie*, ed. Joachim Ritter
(Basel & Stuttgart: Schwabe & Co., 1971), vol. I, pp. 115–117. Martin Heidegger's discussion of Hölderlin's hymn *Andenken* raises problems
which are structurally cognate with the concept of *Ahndung*, which
here is translated as "intuition" and "intuit" respectively.

9. Apparently Hölderlin was about to begin a new paragraph
here; the MS continues on the opposite page with the " Suggestion for
Presentation and Language" which provides the answer to the earlier
question b).

10. This phrase opens Hölderlin's description of the third and
final stage in the dialectical development between spirit and life as
determinants of expression; however, it is interrupted by a long sequence
of parenthetical qualifications ("and finally, after fulfilled . . . ") which
finds its closure with the phrase "—how finally, after this third completion, where . . ." The completion of the main clause is marked by
the new paragraph.

On the Difference of Poetic Modes

1. This text can be dated around summer 1800" (cf. *FE*: vol. 14,
p. 343).

2. The pronoun "these" refers back to "sensuous connection and
assembly" from the main clause.

3. Reference is made to Pindar's 7th Olympian Ode.

4. For the transliteration of *aorgisch* as "aorgic," see note 3 to
"The Ground for Empedocles" above.

5. "*Menin aeide thea.*" Hölderlin cites the opening words of the
Iliad, a text which Hölderlin had studied throughout his studies at the
seminary in Tübingen.

6. This section continues the reflections on the the tragic poem
with which the third long paragraph opened.

7. This table exemplifies essentially the alternation of tones which
the previous sentences elaborated. The abbreviation "p.p." is due to

the belated insertion of the respective lines in which it occurs. According to Beissner (SE: IV, 415) it would be a mistake to neglect this *per procura* and assume that, because of the seemingly identical basic tone and effect, one such tone could be sustained throughout the poem while only its art-character (i.e., the language) be modulated. — The song "Diotima" seems to form an exception to the larger schema. Hence the "?" which Hölderlin puts on the left hand side. For the poem, see SE: I, 227–230.

The Significance of Tragedies

1. The text has to be dated considerably later than the "Homburg period." As is evidenced by the type of paper used by Hölderlin, the sketch was probably written during the time of the Sophocles translations around 1802 (cf. FE: vol. 14, p. 379).

On Religion

1. The date of this text is essentially unclear. Although for different reasons, both the FE and Lawrence Ryan date the text rather early, approximately 1797. The title is Beissner's, and the editors of the FE seem justified in publishing the text under the general heading of "Fragments of Philosophical Letters." Indeed, Hölderlin mentions such a project in a letter to his friend and "philosophical mentor," Immanuel Niethammer, from February 1796 (No. 117, trans. below). While the present translation adheres to the SE, it should be pointed out that the FE (vol. 14, pp. 11–49) reverses parts of this fragmentary text. According to the FE, the text should be read as follows:

Part A From: "[. . .] has to keep, and to this one . . . " until ". . . harmonic whole of modes of life." (This section appears in the SE between pages 278, 1.4 and 279, 1.23.)

Part B From: "You ask me why, even though the people. . ." until ". . . in which those relations existed." (This section opens Beissner's version of the text: SE, pp. 275, 1.2 until 277, 1.27.)

Part C The FE continues the same paragraph with the long sentence "As we already saw, they were right . . . are more inseparably connected." In the SE this sentence is printed as a subtext by Hölderlin (p. 277, 11.30–34).

Part D "And this, then, is the higher enlightenment . . . " continues
in the *FE* with what, in the *SE*, appears as a short fragment
(p. 280, 11.4–12): "[. . .] that is, are such where the
people who exist within them . . . " until ". . . what they
are, and exist undisturbed [. . .]"
Part E Both the *SE* and the *FE* conclude the fragment with the same
paragraphs, starting with "[. . .] hints for continuation."
and ending with ". . . and the destiny of the same), if they
[. . .]."

Whereas Beissner's editorial decisions render the text perhaps
more readable as a whole, although at the possible expense of an overly
rigorous editorial judgment—the decision made by the editors of the
FE to combine this text with the so-called *Älteste Systemprogramm* under
the overall title of *Fragmente Philosophischer Briefe* remains somewhat
unexplained. Given the continuing discussion concerning the authorship of the *Systemprogramm*, it seems, at least for the time being, more
appropriate to keep the two texts apart. For the translation of the
Systemprogramm, see "Appendix" and my introductory note below.

2. Hölderlin renders this sentence in the subjunctive, thus designating, via indirect speech, the hypothetical, speculative nature of
these statements.

3. According to Beissner (*SE*: IV, 417), these lines may be understood either as the closure of the note from the preceding page or as
the last lines of an insertion that was added when the main text had
already been continued.

4. Beissner (*SE*: IV, 417) notes that this is not a heading but
part of a fragmentary sentence.

Becoming in Dissolution

1. According to the *FE*, this text dates around 1800. Again, the
concepts of the title echo Fichte's terminology when he discusses the
formal character of the "reciprocal determination" between "I" and
"non-I" as follows: "The form of reciprocity is no more than the mutual
intrusion, as such, of the components upon each other. The matter is
that in the components which ensures that they can, and must, so
intrude. —The characteristic form of reciprocity in the relation of
efficacy is a *coming-to-be through a passing-away* ["ein Entstehen durch
ein Vergehen"], (a becoming through a disappearance) ["ein Werden
durch ein Verschwinden"]." *Science of Knowledge* (1794–95), 165.

2. The main subject and its appositive never receive their verb; the sentence remains fragmentary.

3. This and several other compound words introduced in this paragraph are quasi-neologisms of Hölderlin. cf. the "truly-tragic" (*echt-tragisch*), the "forever-creative" (*das Immerwährendschöpferische*), the "finite-infinite" (*das Endlichunendliche*), the "individual-eternal" (*das Individuellewige*), "newly-originating" (*das Neuentstehende*).

4. From here on, Hölderlin uses "production" (*Herstellung*) as the antonym for "dissolution"—thus replacing the more Platonic term of "becoming" (*Werden*). When looked at from the "more secure, more relentless and more bold" viewpoint of the "ideal dissolution," all transition possesses the quality of production.

5. I translate *Lebensgefühl* as "sentiment of existence," in deliberate allusion to Rousseau's "Fifth Rêverie." The conception of *Lebensgefühl* which Hölderlin attempts to develop for his own purposes in this essay bears considerable resemblance to Rousseau's argument. For an extensive discussion of the relation between Hölderlin and Rousseau, see Paul de Man's essay, "The Image of Rousseau in the Poetry of Hölderlin."

6. Allusion to Horace, *Odes* III, 29, 11.29f.: "Wisely the God enwraps in fuliginous night/the future's outcome, and laughs . . ." Trans. W. G. Shepherd. (Harmondsworth: Penguin, 1983).

Remarks on Oedipus

1. The "Remarks" on *Oedipus* and *Antigone* were presumably written around September 1803. In a letter to the publisher of his translations, Friedrich Wilmans, Hölderlin states that "these Remarks do not sufficiently express my views of Greek art nor the meaning of the plays" and announces an "Introduction" to the tragedies of Sophocles which, however, he never wrote. (cf. SE: VI, 465; also letters #241 & 243).

The publication of Hölderlin's Sophocles translations is announced in the "*Intelligenzblatt*" No. 112 of the *Hallische Allgemeine Literatur-Zeitung* on July 14, 1805. Friedrich Wilmans speaks of a "classic translation" which "could be considered and recommended as something perfect in its kind" and in which "the philologist [could find] . . . everywhere faithfulness, precision, and the spirit of the German language . . ." (cf. SE: VII,2; 288 f.). However, Hölderlin's translations were generally considered very excentric at best, and even his former colleague Schelling—displaying a rather cold attitude to his old friend from the Tübingen Seminary—writes to Hegel that the translation of Sophocles "expresses most aptly his wasted state of mind" (*SE*: VII,2; 296 f.). The harshest criticism of the translations was voiced by Heinrich Voss (1799–1822), son of the famous Homer translator Johann Heinrich Voss: "[The Meter] is marked by complete lack of character, [the translation] by unlawful boldness and unrestrained fantasy. Occasionally, Mr. Hölderlin stands so high on his elevated position, that of the things beneath him he only perceives faint contours, and that form and determinacy are lost completely . . . How exactly Mr. Hölderlin got up there, we do not quite understand. If he got up there only by accident, then we urge him strongly to very carefully step down to the rest of us. However, if he is up there deliberately and feels at home on those heights, then of course we have to remain silent and only want to have given a warning that nobody attempt to follow him." (*SE*: VII,2; 303 ff.)

For a philologically instructive introduction to these two texts, see the text by Jeremy Adler who also notes that aside from Hölderlin's somewhat imperfect Greek, two poor Greek texts as the basis for Hölderlin's Sophocles translations also marred their success. However, Adler's discussion of Hölderlin's theory of the tragic is marred by a reductive conception of the German notion of *intellektuelle Anschauung*; the term, which Hölderlin explicitly links to tragedy—the latter being its "metaphor"—is not an "intellectual perception" (as Adler translates it). Quite in contrast to any such epistemological and object-determined connotations of the term "perception," Hölderlin's and, in fact, all preceding and subsequent applications of the notion of an "intellectual intuition," involve far more complex considerations. See also the "Introduction" to this translation.

2. *mechane*: Greek for "skill, craft"

3. Hölderlin quotes from his own translation. In the following, I will try to translate his version into English. The differences that emerge between such a rendition and other "Oedipus" translations are, of course, substantial. Also, the lines of Hölderlin's *Oedipus* and *Antigone* are not numbered identically with modern English versions. The line numbers provided in the translation refer to modern printings of the original Greek text.

4. "Nature's scribe, dipping the well-meaning quill." Hölderlin alters a phrase from a Byzantian encyclopedia "that Aristotle was nature's scribe, dipping the quill into meaning;" Hölderlin changes the Greek *eis noun* to *eunoun*, "dipping the well-meaning quill" (cf. *SE*: V, 484).

Dating from the 10th Century and with more than 30,000 entries the largest of its kind, this encyclopedia has been mistakenly attributed to Suidas of Athens. For the complex philological debate concerning the presumably multiple authorship, see *Der Kleine Pauly*. Munich: dtv, 1979. vol. V, 407f.

Remarks on "Antigone"

1. Translation of "das tragischmässige Zeitmatte," a peculiar neologism of Hölderlin. For a possible interpretation of the phrase, cf. Beissner (*SE*: V, 507). Although referring to Beissner, who argues for *-mässig* as meaning not merely "appropriate" (which the German can render more fittingly as *-gemäss*), Jeremy Adler mistranslates the phrase as the "dullness of the time which is *appropriate* to tragedy" (p. 244). Likewise, the pejorative connotations of "dullness" seem questionable, for rather than being the object of a psychological attitude, time, in the sense of temporality, is here veritably constitutive of the dialectic immanent in the tragic. Thus the genetive could be understood as a self-relation (*subjectivus*). Thus Hölderlin argues, in the "Ground for Empedocles," that the subject or tragic hero is indeed "a victim of his time."

2. For the question of translating "*aorgisch*" as "aorgic," see note 3 to "The Ground for Empedocles," above.

3. "Antitheos" here means not simply opposed to the god but also of godlike status.

4. *Dysmoron*: Greek for "bad fate, misfortune."

5. *Prophanethi theos*: "appear oh God!"

No. 41

1. This early letter dates presumably from February 14, 1791.

No. 60

1. Christian Ludwig Neuffer (1769–1839), a good friend of Hölderlin. He entered the Tübingen Seminary in 1786 and remained Hölderlin's close friend until 1800. It seems that Hölderlin saw more talent

in the success-oriented Neuffer (who rose steadily in his career as protestant minister) than is evidenced by the distinctly classicist poetry of
his friend (cf. Beissner, *SE*: VI, 543f.). Hölderlin responds immediately
to Neuffer's letter from July 20, 1793 (cf. *SE*: VII,1; 33 ff.).

2. Gotthold Friedrich Stäudlin (1758–1796), lyric poet and publisher (also of Hölderlin's Hymns), was a leading figure in intellectual
circles of the early Hölderlin. The two poets met in early 1789 (cf.
SE: VII,1; 454). Stäudlin was later expelled as *enragé* because of his
sympathies for the French Revolution and committed suicide in the
Rhine in 1796.

3. Hölderlin's enthusiasm regarding the course of his education
in the Tübingen seminary is specified by a document of a fellow student
who writes: "Together with Hölderlin, Fink, Renz, and other friends,
Hegel read and discussed, following authentic reports, Plato . . . ,
Kant, Jacobi's *Woldemar* and *Allwill* [two philosophical, epistolary nov-
els by Friedrich Heinrich Jacobi (1743–1819)], the Letters on Spinoza
[again by Jacobi], and Hippel's biographies in ascending order [Theodor
Gottlieb von Hippel's (1741–1796) *Biographies* appeared between 1778–
1781]. (cf. *SE*: VII,1; 453 f.)."

4. The letter contains the first, more detailed remarks of Hölderlin on his novel *Hyperion*. The subsequent discussion illustrates his
insecurity with respect to the form of the work. See, the letter to his
brother (No. 97, note 4) below.

5. Reference to Hölderlin's poem "Dem Genius der Kühnheit."

6. Friedrich Matthison (1761–1831), poet and friend of both
Hölderlin, Neuffer, and Stäudlin. M. was present and apparently very
impressed when Hölderlin read to the other two friends his hymn "Dem
Genius der Kühnheit" (cf. Beissner; *SE*: VI, 626).

No. 94

1. Following a recommendation of Stäudlin to Schiller, Hölderlin was a tutor of von Kalb's son between December 1793 and January,
1795 (cf. *SE*: VII,1; 467 ff.). The problems of the teacher-student
relationship rapidly increased since August 1794, and it is in this context that the notion of Hölderlin's insanity surfaces for the first time.
"Many news inform me about the extremely harsh treatment which my
Fritz must tolerate from his teacher.— (I implore you not to let Hölderlin take any note of my knowing this—). His sensitivity is without
limits—and one truly thinks that a disorder of the mind is the foundation

of this behavior" Letter of Charlotte von Kalb to Schiller, Dec. 9, 1794. (*SE*: VII,2; 16 ff).

2. Reference to Schiller's journals *Thalia* and *Die Horen*. Hölderlin had published a first part of his "Hyperion" in *Thalia*.

3. Fichte had published his *Wissenschaftslehre* and his essay on the *Bestimmung des Gelehrten* in 1795; especially the first work was read and studied by Hölderlin with great care. See also his summarizing paragraph of Fichte's work, in particular of the third section, in the letter to his brother (#97), below.

4. For Hölderlin's peculiar interpretation of Fichte's ideas, see Beissner (*SE*: VI, 723 ff.) and the introduction to this translation.

5. Beissner (*SE*: VI, 725) speculates that the gap of five or six lines contained a disclaimer or downtoning of the charges of Fichte's dogmatism.

6. Specifically, Fichte's idea of an infinite progression (*Streben*) was not yet available in reading, since the third part of the *Science of Knowledge* which develops that conception was not published until Easter 1795. It is quite possible, however, that Hölderlin was informed about this crucial part of Fichte's system by way of lectures which he regularly attended.

7. Hegel, who at that time was living in Bern, must have written to Hölderlin about his theological reflections. The most relevant passage, in which Hegel indeed argues for the necessity of a "predestination" as the guiding principle for any proof of God's existence occurs in a fragment which Nohl prints under the general heading "Sketches." "The transcendent Idea of God as the most real being, even if speculative reason was able to prove its reality and existence or capable of evoking a belief in it, would still not be cognizable for us and would not be determinable *qua* itself, unless the contemplation of nature and the concept of an ultimate purpose of the world could be taken as ancillaries." Hegel, *Theologische Jugendschriften*. Ed. Nohl, p. 361 (my translation). However, the fragment is not included in the Kroner translation of Hegel's early writings. See also Hegel's letter to Schelling from January 1795.

No. 97

1. A free quotation of Kant's "categorical imperative."

2. Hölderlin does not quote directly from Fichte but instead offers a strongly condensed summary, particularly of the third part of the

Wissenschaftslehre (cf. Beissner, *SE*: VI, 734f.). This "peculiarity" is already dealt with in Hölderlin's letter to Hegel, No. 94.

3. For Niethammer's *Journal*, cf. letter No. 117, note 1.

4. Schiller writes to his publisher, Cotta: "Hölderlin is writing on a little novel, *Hyperion*, (. . .) I would appreciate if you would take it into print. He has a good deal of genius, and I hope to have some influence on him. I generally count on Hölderlin for *Die Horen* in the future, for he is very hard-working and does not lack the talent to eventually become something in the literary world" (cf. SE: VII,2; 31 f.). Cotta published "Hyperion," paying Hölderlin eventually the rather small sum of 100 Gulden.

No. 117

1. Friedrich Immanuel Niethammer (1766–1848), since 1793 professor of philosophy at the University of Jena, close to Fichte, and founder of the *Philosophisches Journal*, the leading periodical of the time. He knew Hölderlin from the Tübingen seminary and was his friend as well as teacher and philosophical mentor.

2. Karl Leonhard Reinhold (1758–1823), Fichte's predecessor in Jena and known there as a strict follower of Kant through his "Letters about the Kantian Philosophy" (1790–1792).

3. Hölderlin's acceptance of the possibility of an intellectual intuition—already manifest in "Judgment and Being"—marks, despite his well-documented appreciation of Kant, a break with Kant's philosophy. However, Hölderlin's understanding of this concept neither coincides entirely with that of Fichte nor with that of Schelling. For a discussion of Fichte's conception, with which Hölderlin evidently was very familiar (although he seems to misconstrue it), see Ernst Cassirer, *Das Erkenntnisproblem* (vol. III, 137ff.) and my remarks in the introduction to this translation. Regarding Hölderlin's reception of Fichte, see also Ernst Müller, *Hölderlin*, 121ff. and the essays by Dieter Henrich.

4. Schiller's "Letters on the Aesthetic Education of Man" had appeared in his journal *Die Horen* in 1795.

5. Hölderlin apparently refers to the two essays by Schelling, "*Vom Ich als Prinzip der Philosophie* (1795) and *Philosophische Briefe über den Dogmatismus und Kritizismus* which he published in Niethammer's

Journal in 1796. The latter publication is judged favorably by Hölderlin (cf. *SE*: VI, 787). Schelling, after leaving the Seminary in Tübingen in 1795, met with Hölderlin twice in 1795, yet they gradually grew more distant (cf. *SE*: VII,2: correspondence between Hegel and Schelling on Hölderlin: # 145, 146, 165, 166, 167, 312).

No. 121

1. Isaac von Sinclair (1775–1815) first met Hölderlin at Jena in March, 1795. Like Hölderlin, the young democrat and aristocrat Sinclair was fascinated by Fichte, particularly by the ethical implications of his philosophy. He later engaged in various political activities, and was temporarily imprisoned (February to July 1805) after being falsely accused of involvment in a political conspiracy in which Hölderlin, too, was implicated (cf. *SE*: VII, 2; 317–347). Sinclair, who after the loss of his high administrative position in Homburg wrote three philosophical works and who remained in close contact with Hegel, took care of Hölderlin when the poet returned from France in a mentally deranged state in 1802.

No. 172

1. The first part of the letter consists of encouraging words to his brother who apparently was disconcerted with his present existence. However, Hölderlin soon moves on to other concerns. Only at the end of the letter does he make again reference to his brother's personal situation.

2. On Dec. 19, 1798, Hölderlin had published, in the *Allgemeine Zeitung*, a satiric glossary on the excessive amount of lyric poetry in almanacs which "did not decrease (. . .) even though the transcendental speculation (. . .) and politics (. . .) were nothing less than condusive to the bards of the German Parnass" (cf. *SE*: VI, 911).

3. Literally: "captives of their soil," a technical term which originated in the early middle ages, designating the essentially unfree peasant who had to remain on the soil of his feudal lord.

4. The natural philosopher Thales of Milet (624–547 B.C.), and the Athenian statesman and legislator Solon (634–560 B.C.), never travelled together. Hölderlin presumably draws from a chapter in

Diogenes Laertius (approx. third Century A.D.) who wrote a history of famous philosophers and philosophical schools. Diogenes' work also served Hölderlin as his principal source for his *Empedocles*. In a letter to Sinclair, Hölderlin acknowledges his reading of that book (*SE*: VI, 300).

No. 183

1. "The promised:" the idyll "Emilie" for the *Taschenbuch für Frauenzimmer 1800*.

2. Franz Wilhelm Jung (1757–1833) government official in Homburg, later dismissed due to his democratic inclinations, also Mentor of Sinclair. Jung translated Ossian according to a new idea, with a certain regular alternation of tones and rhythms and considered Hölderlin, whom he first met in January 1795, his spiritual mentor. Jung's Ossian translation was eventually published in 1808. (cf. *SE*: VI, 780 and 947).

3. For Böhlendorff, see letters #236 and 240 and note 1 to No. 236 below.

4. For Steinkopf, see the subsequent letter to Schelling and note 3 below.

No. 186

1. After a period of more than three years of silence, Hölderlin attempts to renew his friendship with Schelling. The letter, to be dated for July 1799, not only presents a request for Schelling's participation but also contains an elaboration of Hölderlin's current thinking. Schelling's answer from August 12 was positive. According to Beissner (*SE*: VI, 952f.), Schelling's response evidences that Hölderlin's letter cannot be identical with the one which he eventually mailed. See also Hölderlin's letter to Steinkopf, No. 181 (*SE*: VI, 335f.).

2. For the transliteration of *aorgisch* as "aorgic," see note 3 to the "Ground for Empedocles."

3. Johann Friedrich Steinkopf (1771–1852), a private publisher and antiquarian in Stuttgart, was quite eager to procure contributions from the most prominent literary and philosophical figures of the time. See his letter to Schiller (*SE*: VII,2; 144f.). However, Schiller declined to participate.

4. In his positive response to Hölderlin's proposal, Schelling recommended, however, to abstain from the word "humanity" which, he argued, had come to have a "bad" reputation due to Herder's inflated usage of it (cf. *SE*: VI, 953).

No. 236

1. Casimir Ulrich Böhlendorff (1775–1825), student of law and friend of Hölderlin at least since 1799. His short, erratic and unhappy life was strongly influenced by the revolutionary events in France and Switzerland (Bern, 1798) and by the early German Romantics Wackenroder and Tieck. Böhlendorff failed as a literary figure, and he returned mentally disturbed to his native *Kurland* where he died in 1825 after a life of erratic travels (cf. *SE*, VI, 1074f.).

2. Hölderlin refers to Böhlendorrff's play "Fernando or the Baptizing of Art: A Dramatic Idyll" (1802).

3. "Your Spain" refers to Böhlendorff's play which is set in Spain.

4. A free quotation from Goethe's poem "Die Grenzen der Menschheit."

5. "Otaheiti": island in the South Seas, during Rousseau's era considered a paradise and perhaps known to Hölderlin through travel books.

6. Muhrbeck, Friedrich (1775–1827): friend of Böhlendorf. For a short vita, see *SE*: VI, 900f.

7. Christian Landauer (1769–1845), merchant in Stuttgart who also took a great interest in poetry and music. Landauer arranged the employment as a tutor in Bordeaux, and he also kept regular correspondence with Hölderlin's mother after the poet had returned mentally deranged from Bordeaux in July 1802 (cf. *SE*: VII,1; 169, 178 f. and esp. VII, 2; 174 ff.).

No. 240

1. The letter was written after Hölderlin's return from France, presumably around November 1802 (cf. *SE*: VI, 1086).

2. *Vendée*: coastal region south of the outlet of the Loire. During the years 1793–1796, this area had been the site of a violent insurrection by the Royalist population.

3. "shocks and turmoils." Above all, Hölderlin is referring to the death of his Diotima, Susette Gontard, with whom he had been deeply in love since his stay at the house of the banker Gontard in Frankfurt in 1796.

The Oldest System-Program of German Idealism

1. This fragment, preserved in Hegel's handwriting, was published by the Hegel editor Franz Rosenzweig in 1917 after it had been acquired by the "Königliche Bibliothek Berlin" on an auction. The text was considered a copy and originally attributed to Schelling. In 1926, Hölderlin's first major editor Wilhelm Böhm argued for Hölderlin as the author, and for a long time the consensus on this issue was that Schelling had been the author and yet that the theory of beauty was mainly Hölderlin's work. Recently, Otto Pöggeler has argued that the entire fragment should be attributed to Hegel ("Hegel, der Verfasser des ältesten Systemprogramms des deutschen Idealismus," *Hegel Studien*, Beiheft 4, p. 18). The debate is too complex and, perhaps, not all that important, as to summarize the various positions in greater detail. The fragment is now dated between June and August 1796 (cf. Beissner: SE: IV, 425), a time during which both Hegel and Hölderlin were living in Frankfurt. The editors of the *FE* see great affinities between this fragment and Hölderlin's text "On Religion" and even go so far as to edit both texts together as "Fragmente Philosophischer Briefe" (*FE*: vol. 14, 11 ff.). The question as to when—assuming that the fragment is indeed the result of a sustained exchange between Hölderlin and Schelling—the ideas were first formulated remains unanswerable. Any one of the three meetings between the two thinkers after their common years at the seminary (July–August, 1795, December 1795 in Tübingen; and April 1796 in Frankfurt) may have been the point of conception for the ideas of this fragment.

2. Translation of the composite noun *Buchstabenphilosophen*. The phrase "full of spirit" in the following sentence remains a somewhat imperfect rendering of the German *geistvoll*, a word involving connotations of both, spirit and wit.

Glossary of Terms

Terms marked with an asterisk are also discussed in the notes to the respective text in which they occur; see index.

Ahnden, Ahndung: intuition, intuit*
Anschauung: intuition
Aorgisch vs. *organisch*: aorgic (vs. organic)*
Bedingt, Unbedingt: conditional, unconditional
Bestimmung: determination
Darstellung: presentation
Dichtart: poetic mode
Eigenes, eigentlich: the proper, properly
Empfindung: sensation
Empfindsamkeit: sensitivity
Geist: spirit
Gefühl: sentiment, mood
Gesetzlicher Kalkül: lawful calculation
Grundstimmung, Grundton: basic tone
Idealisch: idealistic
Innigkeit, innig: inwardness, inward
Kalkulables Gesetz: calculable law
Sphäre: sphere*
Urteil: judgment (arche-separation*)
Verstand: understanding
Vorstellung: representation
Vorstellungsform: representational mode
Werden vs. *Vergehen*: becoming vs. dissolution*

Selected Bibliography

Editions of Hölderlin's Works

Hölderlin, Friedrich. *Sämtliche Werke.* (Grosse Stuttgarter Ausgabe), ed. Friedrich Beissner. Stuttgart: Kohlhammer, 1943–1985. Referred to as *SE*.

Hölderlin, Friedrich. *Werke.* (Frankfurter Ausgabe), ed. D. E. Sattler and Wolfram Goddeck. Frankfurt: Verlag Roter Stern, 1975–.

Primary Philosophical Texts (as cited in the Introduction and notes to the translation)

Fichte, Johann G. *Grundlage der gesamten Wissenschaftslehre.* (1794–95) *Gesamtausgabe.* ed. Reinhardt Lauth and Hans Jacob. Stuttgart, Bad-Cannstatt: Friedrich Frommann, 1965. (vol. I,2)

———. "Rezension des Aenesidemus." ibid., vol. I, 2.

———. "Review of Aenesidemus." *Between Kant and Hegel* (Texts in the Development of Post-Kantian Idealism). Trans. and ed. George di Giovanni & H. S. Harris. Albany: State University of New York Press, 1985.

———. "Die Bestimmung des Gelehrten." (1795). *Gesamtausgabe.* vol. I, 3. Bad Cannstatt: Friedrich Frommann, 1966.

———. *The Science of Knowledge.* (1795). Transl. Peter Heath and John Lachs. New York: Appleton-Century-Crofts, 1970.

184

Hegel, Georg F. W. *Theologische Jugendschriften*. Ed. Herman Nohl. (Tübingen: 1907). Reprint: Frankfurt: Minerva, 1966.

————. *Early Theological Writings*. Trans. T. M. Knox. Introd. and Transl. of fragments by R. Kroner. Chicago: Univ. of Chicago Press, 1948.

Hemsterhuis, Frans. "Lettre sur les désirs." *Oeuvres Philosophiques*. (1846). Reprint: Hildesheim: Georg Olms, 1972.

Herder, J. G. "Liebe und Selbstheit." *Sämtliche Werke*. Ed. B. Suphan. (1877–1913). Reprint, Hildesheim: Georg Olms, 1967. vol. XV, 304–326.

Kant, Immanuel. *Kritik der Praktischen Vernunft* (1788). & "Grundlegung zur Metaphysik der Sitten" (1785). *Werkausgabe*, vol. VII. ed. Wilhelm Weisschedel. Frankfurt: Suhrkamp, 1982.

————. *Kritik der Urteilskraft*. (1790). *Werkausgabe*, vo. X. Frankfurt: Suhrkamp, 1981.

————. "Mutmassliche Anfänge der Menschheitsgeschichte." *Werkausgabe* vol. 11. 85–102.

————. *Critique of Practical Reason*. Trans. Lewis W. Beck. Indianapolis: Bobbs Merrill, 1956.

————. *Grounding for the Metaphysics of Morals*. Trans. James W. Ellington. Indianapolis & London: Hackett, 1981.

————. *Critique of Judgment*. Trans. J. H. Bernard. New York: Hafner, 1951.

————. "Conjectural Beginning of Human History." Trans. Emil L. Fackenheim. *On History*. Ed. Lewis W. Beck. Indianapolis: Bobbs Merrill, 1957. 52–68.

Schelling, Friedrich W. J. "Vom Ich als Prinzip der Philosophie oder über das Unbedingte im menschlichen Wissen." (1795) *Schellings Werke*, ed. Manfred Schröter. Munich: Beck, 1923. vol. I.

————. "Philosophische Briefe über den Dogmatismus und Kritizismus." (1796), ibid. vol. I.

————. *System des Transzendentalen Idealismus* (1800), ibid. vol. III.

————. *System of Transcendental Idealism* (1800). Trans. Peter Heath. Charlottesville: University Press of Virginia, 1978.

Schiller, Friedrich. "Über die Aesthetische Erziehung des Menschen, in einer Reihe von Briefen." (1795). *Sämtliche Werke*. ed. Benno von Wiese. Weimar: Herman Bohlau, 1962. vol. XX.

————. *On the aesthetic education of man, in a series of letters*. Trans. Elizabeth M. Wilkinson and L. A. Willoughby. Oxford: Clarendon, 1967.

————. "Über Anmut und Würde". *Sämtliche Werke*, vol. XX, 251–308.

Critical Writings on Hölderlin and Related Issues

Adler, Jeremy. "On Tragedy: 'Notes on the Oedipus' and 'Notes on the Antigone'." (Translation of Hölderlin's Notes with an Introduction). *Comparative Criticism*. 5 (1983): 205–244.

Allemann, Beda. *Hölderlin und Heidegger*. (Zürich & Freiburg: Atlantis, 1954).

Beissner, Friedrich. *Hölderlins Übersetzungen aus dem Griechischen*. (1933) Stuttgart: Metzler, 1961.

Berlinger, Rudolph. "Hölderlin's Philosophische Denkart" in *Eupherion* 62 (1968): 1–12.

Bernd, Clifford A. "The Formal Qualities of Hölderlin's 'Wink für Darstellung und Sprache" in *Modern Language Review*, 60 (1965): 400–404.

Binder, Wolfgang. "Hölderlins Tragödienverständnis" in *Kleist Jahrbuch* (1981–82): 33–49.

Blanchot, Maurice, "Recherches: Le Tournant" in *Nouvelle Revue Francaise*, vol. 5 (1955): 110–120.

Broecker, Walter. "Zu Hölderlins Oedipus Deutung" in: *Martin Heidegger zum siebzigsten Geburtstag*. Pfullingen: Neske, 1959.

Brown, Marshall. "The Eccentric Path." *JEGP* 77 (1978): 104–112.

Buddeberg, Else, "Hölderlins Begriff der 'Receptivität des Stoffs.'" In *Germanisch Romanische Monatsschrift* 43 (1962): 170–193.

Cassirer, Ernst. Hölderlin und der Deutsche Idealismus. in: *Idee und Gestalt*. (1922) Darmstadt: Wissenschaftliche Buchgesellschaft, 1981. 113–155.

Corngold, Stanley. "Hölderlin and the Interpretation of the Self." *Comparative Criticism* 5 (1983): 187–200.

Corssen, Meta, "Die Tragödie als Begegnung zwischen Gott und Mensch: Hölderlins Sophocles-Deutung." In *Hölderlin Jahrbuch* vol. 3 (1948–49): 139–187.

De Man, Paul. The Image of Rousseau in the Poetry of Hölderlin. In *The Rhetoric of Romanticism*. New York: Columbia Univ. Press, 1984. 19–45.

———. "Wordsworth and Hölderlin." In: *The Rhetoric of Romanticism*, 47–65.

———. "Intentional Structure of the Romantic Image," *Rhetoric of Romanticism*, 1–17.

Erdmann, Veronika. *Hölderlins Ästhetische Theorie*. Jena: Frommann, 1923.

Gaier, Ulrich. *Der Gesetzliche Kalkül*. Tübingen: Niemeyer, 1962.

———. Stoff und Geist: Untersuchungen zum ersten Satz von Hölderlin's Aufsatz "Über die Verfahrungsweise des Poetischen Geistes." In *Dimensionen der Sprache in der Philosophie des Deutschen Idealismus*, ed. Brigitte Scheer, Günter Wohlfahrt. Würzburg: Königshausen & Neumann, 1982. 88–109.

Gaskill, Howard. "Some Recent Trends in Hölderlin Criticism." *German Life and Letters* 36 (1982–83): 166–181.

Heidegger, Martin. *Erläuterungen zu Hölderlin's Dichtung.* Frankfurt: Klosterman, 1981.

———. *Hölderlins Hymnen "Germanien" und "Der Rhein."* Frankfurt: Klostermann, 1980.

———. *Hölderlins Hymne "Andenken."* Frankfurt: Klostermann, 1982.

———. *Hölderlins Hymne "Der Ister."* Frankfurt: Klostermann, 1984.

Henrich, Dieter. *Hölderlin über Urteil und Sein.* (Eine Studie zur Entwicklungsgeschichte des deutschen Idealismus), *Hölderlin Jahrbuch,* vol. 14 (1965–66): 73–96.

———. "Hegel und Hölderlin." *Hegel im Kontext.* Frankfurt: Suhrkamp, 1971, 9–40.

———. "Über Hölderlins philosophische Anfänge. Im Anschluss an die Publikation eines Blattes in Niethammers Stammbuch." *Hölderlin Jahrbuch* vol. 24 (1984–85): 1–28.

Jamme, Christoph. "'Jedes Lieblose ist Gewalt': Der junge Hegel, Hölderlin und die Dialektik der Aufklärung." *Hölderlin Jahrbuch.* vol. 23 (1982–83): 191–228.

Kondylis, Panajotis. *Die Entstehung der Dialektik.* (Eine Analyse der geistigen Entwicklung von Hölderlin, Schelling und Hegel bis 1802). Stuttgart: Klett Cotta, 1979.

Konrad, Michael. *Hölderlins Philosophie im Grundriss.* (Analytisch-Kritischer Kommentar zu Hölderlins Aufsatzfragment "Über die Verfahrungsweise des Poetischen Geistes"). Bonn: Bouvier, 1967.

Kurz, Gerhard. *Mittelbarkeit und Vereinigung.* (Zum Verhältnis von Poesie, Reflexion und Revolution bei Hölderlin). Stuttgart: Metzler, 1975.

Lacoue-Labarthe, Philippe. "The Cesura of the Speculative." *Glyph* 4 (1978): 57–84.

———. "Hölderlin et les Grecs." *Poétique* vol. 40 (1979): 465–474.

Lang, Dieter. "Die Erhebung zum 'höheren' Leben: Eine Problemskizze zu Hölderlins Aufsatz "Über Religion." *Philosophische Perspektiven*, ed. Rudolph Beringer and Eugen Fink. Frankfurt: 1972.

Liebruck, Bruno. *Die Sprache Hölderlins in der Spannweite von Mythos und Logos, Wirklichkeit und Realität* Bern, Frankfurt, Las Vegas: 1979.

Mieth, Günther. *Friedrich Hölderlin: Dichter der bürgerlich-demokratischen Revolution.* Berlin: Rutten & Loenig, 1978.

Müller, Ernst. *Hölderlin: Studien zur Geschichte seines Geistes.* Stuttgart and Berlin: Kohlhammer, 1944.

Nägele, Rainer. *Literatur und Utopie.* Heidelberg: Lothar Stiem, 1978.

———. *Hölderlin: Text, Geschichte, und Subjektivität.* Stuttgart: Metzler, 1985.

Pellegrini, Allesandro. *Friedrich Hölderlin: Sein Bild in der Forschung.* Trans. Christoph Gassner. Berlin: De Gruyter, 1965.

Read, Ralph R. "On the Process of the Poetic Mind." (Trans. of "Über die Verfahrungsweise des Poetischen Geistes"). *German Romantic Criticism*, ed. Leslie Wilson. New York: Continuum, 1982. 219–237.

Ryan, Lawrence J. *Hölderlin's Lehre vom Wechsel der Töne*, Stuttgart: Kohlhammer, 1960.

Seebass, Friedrich. "Hölderlins Sophocles-Übertragungen im zeitgenössischen Urteil." *Philologus* vol. 77 (1921): 413–21.

Strack, Friedrich. *Aesthetik und Freiheit.* (Hölderlins Idee von Schönheit, Sittlichkeit und Geschichte in der Frühzeit). Tübingen: Niemeyer, 1976.

Szondi, Peter. "Hölderlin-Studien" in *Schriften I.* Frankfurt: Suhrkamp, 1978. 287–418.

———. "Hölderlin's Overcoming of Classicism." Trans. Timothy Bahti. *Comparative Criticism* 5 (1983): 251–270.

————. *On Textual Understanding and Other Essays.* Trans. Harvey Mendelsohn. Minneapolis: University of Minnesota Press, 1986.

Thomasberger, Andreas. "'Der Gesichtspunct aus dem wir das Altertum anzusehen haben.' Grundlinien des Hölderlinschen Traditionsverständnisses." *Hölderlin Jahrbuch,* vol. 24 (1984–85): 189–194.

Van de Velde, Leonardus, *Herrschaft und Knechtschaft bei Hölderlin.* Assen: Van Gorcum & Comp. B.V., 1973.

Warminski, Andrzej. "Hölderlin in France." *Studies in Romanticism,* 22 (1983): 173–197.

Index

Works are indexed under their authors